AUTHENTIC

AUTHENTIC

DEVELOPING THE DISCIPLINES OF A SINCERE FAITH

JAMES MacDONALD

MOODY PUBLISHERS

CHICAGO

Published in association with the literary agency of Wolgemuth and Associates, Inc.

Edited by Neil Wilson
Cover Design: Michael Ranville/Walk In the Word
Cover Illustration: Nolan Abbey and Nate Baron
Interior Design: Smartt Guys design

Library of Congress Cataloging-in-Publication Data

MacDonald, James, 1960-
 Authentic : developing the disciplines of a sincere faith / James MacDonald.
  p. cm.
 Includes bibliographical references (p.   ).
 ISBN 978-0-8024-5724-0 hdbk
 ISBN 978-0-8024-5717-2 ppbk
 1. Spiritual life--Christianity. 2. Christian life. I. Title.
 BV4501.3.M2325 2013
 248.4--dc23
                2012035680

We hope you enjoy this book from Moody Publishers. Our goal is to provide high-quality, thought-provoking books and products that connect truth to your real needs and challenges. For more information on other books and products written and produced from a biblical perspective, go to www.moodypublishers.com or write to:

Moody Publishers
820 N. LaSalle Boulevard
Chicago, IL 60610

Moody Publishers is committed to caring wisely for God's creation and uses recycled paper whenever possible. The paper in this book consists of 30 percent post-consumer waste.

1 3 5 7 9 10 8 6 4 2

Printed in the United States of America

To XLT, some of the most authentic Christians I know:

Fred Adams

Rick Donald

Janine Nelson

Trei Tatum

CONTENTS

got a tattoo. I did it at age 51 and if you don't know me, the decision might surprise you. I got the logo from my recent book *Vertical Church*, inked on my right forearm and I did it on the day I finished the manuscript. Not because I think it's cool or I like the reinforcement of my most important "life message," so readily visible. Not because I'm having a midlife crisis or even because I like tattoos. The decision is actually rooted in something deeper—sort of a "push back," really. The biggest obstacle I faced thirty years ago in becoming a pastor and have battled every step of the way since is how the expectations of congregants near and far pressure you into a mold I never wanted, haven't worn well, and actually repudiate. All of us should conform to the biblical mandate for holiness, but none of us should be forced to fit cultural sensitivities or historic expectations not found in God's Word.

My one determination when I surrendered to God's call upon my life was that I would be true to the way God made me and not lose my off-beat sense of humor or my sometimes zany and unpredictable pursuit of fun. Incredibly, my highest goal at age twenty-two, fresh out of Bible college, was not to be a man of faith or a pastor of great influence. My deepest determination was to be absolutely and always authentic. Yes, godly and biblical, of course; holy and humble by God's grace—but in it all I deeply desired to be authentic. Not fake or phony—not a guy who publicly phones it in, while in private his heart is far from God. And hopefully never a person who conforms to the pressures others collectively put on us. So my tattoo points to the only reliable place of external pressure to conform—to the Lord above. It's a reminder to me that I live for an audience of One and, and in the end, only His view of our authenticity matters. If you long to be authentic, I think you'll love this book.

Authentic is one of those words we use to describe a life worth living. It's a person *being themselves* (or who they are meant to be) in the best sense of the idea. Genuine human beings are people we almost instinctively want to emulate. But authentic people are often hard to find.

So before we go any further, let's define *authentic* so we will have an agreed picture in mind as we explore the spiritual disciplines that can help us live a genuine, sincere faith. Authentic: the original article, the real thing, not a phony, knockoff, or cheap imitation. Authentic doesn't necessarily mean *unique*. A craftsman may produce many authentic pieces. In usage, we often mean by authentic that the object conforms to an original ideal or pattern so as to faithfully reproduce the essential features. The denim jeans featured on the cover of this book are known for their style, weight, and durability. We're not looking for an inferior imitation—we're looking for the real thing in a size that fits us. When something is authentic, we expect it to be actually and exactly what it is claimed to be. So an authentic piece of Early American furniture cannot have been built last week, but an authentic reproduction based on accurate measurements of a classic original may well have been assembled recently. A faithful copy can be called authentic as long as it's not called original. We're accustomed to having the word *authentic* used in describing products or even experiences; but when it comes to people, not so much.

Becoming an authentic person is an easy goal to claim; it's harder to live out under scrutiny. This book is about developing and doing the spiritual disciplines of a sincere faith. Committed Christians across the centuries have demonstrated that there are certain practices that can lead to a deepening and sharpening of our likeness to Christ. This book is *not* about frantic performance to prove a point. Authenticity isn't forced. As we will see, human authenticity includes room for failure. Admission of error and genuine repentance are definitely marks of authenticity.

Our standard for authenticity is Jesus Christ. He's the real original. This is true because He is not only our Maker and therefore qualified to tell us how to live authentically, He is also our ultimate model.[1] Humanly speaking, He was in every way our perfect example. In fact, the Christian life could be described as learning to live faithfully as an authentic imitation of Jesus. That's why the apostle Peter, no stranger to hard lessons and humiliating failures, and who was told

> THE MORE WE CAN BE LIKE JESUS, THE MORE WE WILL BE LIVING AN AUTHENTIC LIFE.

in no uncertain terms by Jesus **"You follow me,"**[2] passed on that same wisdom to us: **"For to this you have been called, because Christ also suffered for you, leaving you an example, so that you might follow in his steps."**[3] We can't duplicate what Jesus did, but we can imitate Him. *The more we can be like Jesus, the more we will be living an authentic life.*

The disciplines of a sincere faith featured in this book are practical ways to **"follow in his steps."** Authentic Christians don't drift in His steps, or wander in roughly the same direction as His steps—we *follow in His steps.* Each of these disciplines was taught and exemplified by Jesus. That's how we know they are worth pursuing. When we are practicing them rightly, we are setting our feet in His footprints. This is why a book on developing the disciplines of a sincere faith begins with a chapter on identifying the habits of hypocritical people. There's some stuff we're going to have to leave behind if we are really going to **"follow in his steps."**

When the apostle Paul was training up his protégé Timothy in the disciplines of faith, he didn't end until he established a healthy standard for the young disciple. That standard wasn't perfection; it was persistence: **"Practice these things, immerse yourself in them, so that *all may see your progress.* Keep a close watch on yourself and on the teaching.**

Persist in this, for by so doing you will save both yourself and your hearers."[4] If you and I aim at authentic perfection, it only takes about fifteen seconds to fall short. If we aim at genuine progress, if we are willing to let God keep working on us as long as it takes, and no matter what it takes, things happen. People already know you won't be perfect, so don't waste time trying to prove otherwise. But they will pay attention when they see progress in your life. The authentic Christian life is compared to a journey and a long race. Following Jesus is the ultimate marathon, and the more we incorporate the spiritual disciplines in our running the life, the more we will cross the finish line *accelerating*!

Let me pray for all of us as we embark together on this tour of the disciplines of a sincere faith:

Father, if we are imitations of one thing, may it be of Your Son, Jesus. You have called us out of darkness and into light. You have raised us through Your Son from death in sin to life in Him. I pray this is clearly true of each reader of these words, and if not, that he or she would in this moment be strongly convicted by Your Spirit of the crucial need to surrender to You even before embarking on these disciplines. Help us to remember that these practices are never a means to salvation but an evidence that we are working out the salvation You have freely given us in Christ.

Lord, help us understand that You are more committed to training us up into these disciplines than we are. You want to energize us by Your Spirit and make us wise in Your Word to undertake these exercises in sanctification. You are doing and will do the good work in us. Again, to borrow Paul's words, may we be diligent in this pursuit: " **. . . work out your own salvation with fear and trembling, for God it is who works in you, both to will and to work for his good pleasure."**[5] *Thank You for being willing to enter our lives to create in each of us an authentic imitation of Your Son. We know it is the kind of work that only You can do. We want to be willing to let You every step of the way. In Jesus' name, Amen.*

HOW TO GET THE MOST
OUT OF *AUTHENTIC*

T he subtitle of this book is *Developing the Disciplines of a Sincere Faith*. This is intended as an accurate description as well as a promise. To be what an authentic Christian is, you must do what an authentic Christian does. To that end, I have incorporated several features in this book designed to maximize your willingness to develop certain disciplines of a sincere faith in Jesus Christ.

THE BIBLE IN *AUTHENTIC*

It has become my practice to place quoted Scripture in **bold font** in my books. I want the Word of God to stand out among my words. I also want my readers to have every opportunity to compare what God says with any comments or teaching I write. Ideally, you will read *Authentic* with your Bible open—practicing the discipline of shaping and checking your thinking and life with Scripture. Bible study is one of the specific disciplines of a sincere faith that we will examine in these pages, but this entire book can be an exercise for you in that discipline, as you note how the Bible is used as the source for every insight and the authority behind the teaching.

THE REAL THING

Before chapters 2–7, I've included a personal testimony of the way God has dealt in my own life regarding the discipline you are about to consider. After the manuscript of the book was prepared, I sat and considered the impact of these disciplines on my life. I'm not claiming any special dispensation of authenticity, but I want you to know that I've wrestled with and learned about these spiritual disciplines in the trenches of life, ministry, and my personal walk with God. Where I've found some victory and progress, I am fully and deeply aware that God's grace has been operating in ways well beyond even the ones that are abundantly apparent to me. I trust you will be instructed by my failures and encouraged by the lessons I've been taught.

PRACTICING THE DISCIPLINES

I have included throughout the chapters a number of applications that I trust will be helpful to you as you begin or continue to exercise these disciplines in your life. I can assure you that time and effort invested in these disciplines will generate benefits. I have tried to give you some idea of what those might be with each discipline. What I don't want you to expect is immediate success and awestruck wonder by those around you at your sudden aura of "glow in the dark" Jesus. For purposes of accountability, you may want to let one or two people know about your intentions in this area. Though most people in your life shouldn't know *why* things are changing, they should be able to see some changes in you.

One of the noticeable effects of taking the spiritual disciplines seriously is that people may recognize your life is no longer drifting along, sensing a new direction and purpose. You are beginning to take steps in life as God intended rather than letting the pressures and tides of the world determine where your life is going. But here's a warning: the most immediate experience you have when you embark on any of these spiritual disciplines is *resistance*. The "old" you won't want to make these changes. Some people in your life will not want you to alter your behavior (if for no other reason than your progress will convict them about their own lives). And the world and powers that control it for now will not welcome disciplined spiritual change on your part, either. But let me remind you of some of Jesus' closing words that we specially need to remember when we find ourselves thinking that the point of following Him was just to make our lives wonderful and easy: **"I have said these things to you, that in me you may have peace. In the world you will have tribulation. But take heart; I have overcome the world."**[6]

Welcome to another chapter in the life adventure of developing the disciplines of a sincere faith. Follow in His steps.

CHAPTER ONE

SEVEN HABITS OF
HIGHLY HYPOCRITICAL PEOPLE

et's be authentic! I'm as anxious as you are about digging into what it means to be real people, but experience tells me that we can't start examining *authenticity* until we've confronted *hypocrisy*. We won't take seriously the practices of a sincere faith until we see the danger of insincerity. And believe me, there is a lot of pretense out there. All of us know people who wear masks; acting like they're something they're not. But if we're not careful, hypocrisy is an easy act to put on ourselves.

It would be massively hypocritical and truly inauthentic of me to race into this subject without stopping to disclose my own battles with hypocrisy. While, by God's grace, there is nothing "behind the curtain" that would make you want to throw this book in the fireplace, I have had seasons in my life since high school where my "public" outpaced my "private" and led inevitably to relational fallout and bitter tears. Like Peter after his 3-peat denial **"went out and wept bitterly,"**[1] I have felt the sting of being *for* Christ and others *far less* than I desired to be. I have lost my cool with treasured staff. I have struggled to forgive when extended family has hurt me, and I have neglected my wife and kids for brief periods when the demands of opportunity outshouted personal sanity. I have seen a few things a man of God should not look at and handled pressure in ways that protected self instead of honoring others. I have even had some seasons where my neglect of the disciplines included here has ravaged my soul, requiring me to crawl back for fresh mercy and renewed pursuit. What I have never done, by God's grace, is refuse His discipline, or harden my heart to His calls for humility, confession, and reconciliation, both vertically (with Him) and horizontally (with others).

Nothing will shred your soul faster than acceptance of hypocrisy, so let's deal head-on with the matter of this authentic opposite. We can't read Matthew 23 attentively without feeling just a little uncomfortable, because Jesus didn't mince words when it came to hypocrisy. He went hard after it. The language of this passage is unparalleled in all of the words that came from the mouth of Jesus Christ.

The first verses are a backdrop for everything that happens: **"Then Jesus said to the crowds and to his disciples, 'The scribes and the Pharisees sit on Moses' seat . . .'"** (vv. 1–2). In other words, Jesus recognized that the current religious leaders had inherited Moses's authority. They were supposed to be guardians of the Law, not reshapers of God's instruction. They had no license to revise or rewrite what God said.

Once Jesus acknowledged the leaders' position, He cautioned about thoughtless obedience: **". . . so practice and observe whatever they tell you, but not the works they do. For they preach, but do not practice"** (v. 3). The Pharisees could quote Scripture with the best of them; but their personal lives were a contradiction, not to be imitated. **"They tie up heavy burdens** (one translation says, 'They bind up'), **hard to bear, and lay them on people's shoulders, but they themselves are not willing to move them with their finger"** (v. 4). Picture someone filling a large backpack with rocks, tying odd but heavy stuff all over the outside of the pack, and then instructing you to pick it up and carry it joyfully while they stand back and watch you stagger down the road.

"They do all their deeds to be seen by others" (v. 5). The Pharisees were famous for putting on a good show in public while they exempted themselves from their own rules in private. Failure of integrity at the leadership level leads to a casual and even arrogant attitude toward integrity at other levels. *If the leaders can get away with this stuff, why not the rest of us?* Unchallenged, sham-living at the top results in sham-living all the way to the bottom!

"For they make their phylacteries ..." (v. 5). Devout Jewish people wore special headbands with a little box attached that looked like a headlamp. Inside were small scrolls with meticulously copied portions of Scripture. Their outfits were ostentatious, showing all who saw them they were set apart and special. "I love the Bible so much I'm wearing it!"

> OVER THE CENTURIES, THE ISRAELITES TRANSFORMED DEUTERONOMY 6:8 FROM A VIVID COMMAND INTO A HOLLOW REENACTMENT OF GOD'S TRUTH.

Over the centuries, the Israelites transformed Deuteronomy 6:8 from a vivid command into a hollow reenactment of God's truth. The entire context was about God's law and the fact that it was supposed to be the subject of continual meditation, conversation, and obedience:

> **And these words that I command you today shall be on your heart. You shall teach them diligently to your children, and shall talk of them when you sit in your house, and when you walk by the way, and when you lie down, and when you rise. You shall bind them as a sign on your hand, and they shall be as frontlets between your eyes. You shall write them on the doorposts of your house and on your gates.[2]**

Instead of being *as* signs or *as* frontlets (as in, *always immediately accessible to you*), snippets of God's laws had become trinkets worn for show. The symbols had replaced what they were intended to symbolize. Today's version might be, *I love God's Word—I own fifteen Bibles—but no, I don't actually read any of them.*

Jesus continued in Matthew 23:6–7, **". . . and they love the place of honor at feasts and the best seats in the synagogues and greetings in the marketplaces and being called rabbi by others."** Their role as teachers had become all about them and the prestige that went with the position rather than their responsibility before God! Jesus shifted the emphasis back where it belonged. **"But you are not to be called rabbi, for you have one Teacher, and you are all brothers"** (v. 8). The messenger is nothing; the message is everything. **"And call no man your father on earth . . ."** No religious leader is to be called father. How clear is that? Don't call people "father" for **". . . you have one Father who is in heaven"** (v. 9).

"Neither be called instructors, for you have one instructor, the Christ. The greatest among you shall be your servant. Whoever exalts himself will be humbled, and whoever humbles himself will be exalted" (vv. 10–12). Now as Jesus was saying these things (remember from verse 1) to the crowds and to His disciples, the scribes and the Pharisees were listening in. And their mouths were falling open. Then Jesus turned His attention toward them directly and used the strongest language of denunciation in the entire New Testament to address Himself to the subject of hypocrisy.

Jesus said, **"But woe to you, scribes and Pharisees. . . ."** He will repeat that word *woe* seven times in the verses that follow. The Greek *ouai* is not so much a word but a heart cry of anger, pain, and denunciation. It expresses grief and profound dissatisfaction. Yet here, from the lips of Christ, it's not an *exclamation*, as in "Whoa!" or a point of punctuation; it is a divine *proclamation* of judgment. As the second person of the Trinity, Jesus pronounces God's verdict upon the hypocrites and points to their sentencing in eternity.

The word *woe* on Jesus' lips that day meant, "How *greatly* you will suffer!" So when Jesus Christ says multiple times, beginning in verse 13, "Woe to you," we can't read those phrases softly or casually. It's "WOE to you, scribes and Pharisees!"

The Pharisees Jesus was chastising were the most religious people of their day. They were the Bible-carrying believers, the most *into it* of anyone. And if you consider yourself *into* God's Word as I do, then we—more than any others—are the possible contemporary parallel for the Pharisees. Of course their error was not their reverence for God's Word but their insistence upon adding to parts while ignoring others. We must check ourselves against the standard Jesus used.

Jesus was confronting men who were serious—even fanatical about their man-made religion. I could go on at length about the Pharisees, Sadducees, and the scribes, but I fear an extended description would be a distraction from the application of the message. Our goal is not to learn how hypocritical the religious leaders of Jesus' day were but to get a mirror and examine ourselves. Let me say at the outset that I have been thoroughly worked over by God's Spirit in the preparation of this chapter and have not failed in my search for significant areas of hypocrisy in my own life—gaps between what I want to be and what I actually am. I encourage you to do the same as you read.

Matthew 23:13 says, **"But woe to you, scribes and Pharisees, hypocrites!"** The word *hypocrite* is such a powerful term that instead of trying to translate it, we've simply borrowed it from Greek (*hupocrites*) into English. The expression originated from theatric practices in ancient times where actors wore masks rather than makeup in order to hide their true identities. So much so, that the word *hypocrite* was originally a compliment for actors with theatrical skills. We are all familiar with Hollywood stars who can vividly portray a beautiful, loving, selfless family. And then we learn that they are the very *opposite* in real life. They can act a role convincingly, but they are not truly the person they pretend to be. That disconnect between a part well played and a life poorly lived became the meaning of *hypocrite*—one who portrays himself to be what he is not. We are hypocrites when we assume a position of piety when in reality we are destitute of genuine faith; acting the part of being close to God when our heart is very far from Him.

Jesus said of the Pharisees, **"[They] honor me with their lips, but their heart is far from me."**[3] This phrase describes the general attitude behind what I call the *Seven Habits of Highly Hypocritical People*. As we go through these seven characteristics, I want to encourage you to ask yourself these questions: *Am I like that? Do I do that?* Jot your self-assessment down in the margin beside each characteristic. Let me warn you that no one is entirely exempt from areas of personal hypocrisy. Admitting inconsistencies is a good sign, because none of us have arrived. I would be concerned about a person who could read this chapter and not experience a single moment of personal conviction about falling short of what we profess. We are all, to one degree or another, hypocrites or liars. It's one of the marks that confirm we are fallen human beings desperately in need of God's forgiveness and grace.

The Pharisees were spiritually and ethically blind. We are *all* like them to a certain extent when it comes to our own shortcomings. But we need a mirror that will show us who we really are[4] and set us free. We can't give ourselves sight. Honest, accurate reflection is a miracle done by the Holy Spirit, bringing the truths of Scripture to bear upon our souls; God's Word wiping away the false and hypocritical.

Before we can move forward in the *process* of becoming authentic, we must have the *crisis* of facing what lacks. How can we work through chapters on developing the solutions to a problem we don't yet acknowledge? So that's the point of this chapter, to let God take away the masks of hypocrisy keeping us from being who He wants us to be. Our masks of hypocrisy are the habits of our lives that parallel the Pharisees' offenses.

» Habit One: Making salvation as complicated as possible.

"But woe to you, scribes and Pharisees, hypocrites! For you shut the kingdom of heaven in people's faces."[5] The expression **"the kingdom of heaven"** is a reference to salvation; entrance into God's family. A hypocritical believer has the habit of making salvation as complicated as possible.

Salvation is not easy, but it is simple. It costs everything, but it's uncomplicated. Jesus said it is so simple that even a child can understand it.[6] Someone very young can grasp the gospel that God loves sinners and that we need His forgiveness. They can put their faith in Jesus Christ who died to pay the penalty for our sins. Even a small child can receive Christ by faith. That's the gospel.

It's not easy (it wasn't easy for Jesus to provide our salvation and it's not easy to turn away from pride and sin to receive the gift with open hands), but it's simple. Hypocrites go out of their way to make it complicated. *"You've got to do these fifteen things. You've got to follow these steps to enlightenment—maybe. You've got to go through these seven sacraments perfectly or you can't be saved. And if the system fails, it's your fault. And you had better come to church and keep all the rules."*

Hypocrites leverage people into religion and out of personal relationship with Jesus Christ, the power and the simplicity of the gospel. Paul said to the Corinthians, **"I fear . . . your minds may somehow be corrupted from the simplicity that is in Christ."**[7] Hypocrites, though? Their attitude and response if someone should ask, "What must I do to be saved?" is, "It's complicated . . ." Talk about shutting the kingdom in someone's face! I love the kind of testimony that reveals people who want to share the joy of salvation with others. All it takes is one person reaching out to another person in love. The invitation can be as simple and direct as, "You know, I want to pray with you to receive Christ as Savior and Lord." That's what sincere people do: love and care for those who are lost and hurting, while not making it some religious complicated you've-got-to-do-all-these-87-things to get the free gift. What a tragedy when people accept Christ simply and then gradually come to view the gospel as something so complex they don't pass it on. *I got saved but I can't possibly tell you how to get it. It's so complicated, I might get it wrong.* God help us to keep the message of Christ's love and forgiveness simple and available to everyone. Anything else is hypocrisy.[8]

» Habit Two: Getting what I need from people even if it hurts them.
Christ said this: **"Woe to you, scribes and Pharisees, hypocrites!
For you devour widows' houses and for a pretense you make long
prayers. Therefore, you will receive the greater condemnation."**[9]
The idea behind the word *devour* is, *"you consume for personal gain,"* like a
wild dog eats a rabbit. Jesus said, **"You devour widows' houses."** The
word *widows* represents those with many needs and few resources. We are
challenged throughout Scripture to care for the widows in our church, to
love them, to help them out. Everyone who has many hardships and few
resources is our responsibility.[10] But a hypocrite does the opposite. Jesus
was describing a religious person seeing someone in poverty then going
and devouring the little bit they have out of an arrogant sense of, "Even
though you don't have much, God wants me to have your meager supply
for my uses." It's the idea of personal gain even if it hurts others, which
brings us to the second part of this highly hypocritical habit.

Jesus goes on, **"Woe to you, scribes and Pharisees, hypocrites! For you
travel across sea and land** (go way out of your way) **to make a single proselyte** (convert), **and when he becomes a proselyte, you make him twice as
much a child of hell as yourselves."**[11] Can you believe Christ said that?

"That's not my mild-mannered Jesus . . ."

Well, this *is* Christ speaking. This is who He is. He pulls out the big
guns for hypocrisy. **"Man looks at the outward appearance, but the
LORD looks on the heart."**[12] Jesus was doing a spiritual electrocardio-
gram on the Pharisees and the results were not good. Supposed spiritual
leaders but so consumed with self: *"My situation, my needs, my desires, and
my plans. And if I don't get my way, don't cross me. Don't show me up or you'll pay
for it."* Hypocrites hurt people; they don't help them. They do damage in
the name of God. That's not the heart of a Christian.

I have to live with the memory of how often I have hurt people without
meaning to while leading our church through the years. I've done things
I could have done better. I've made difficult decisions that had to be made
that I know hurt people, but were in the interests of what God was doing

in our church. But every time—regardless of whether the error was mine or theirs—I have felt deep grief in knowing someone was injured.

But unintended hurt is not what Jesus is talking about—the way truth sometimes hurts, or the ways we sometimes unintentionally hurt people. **"We all stumble in many ways."**[13] He *is* talking about people who callously and indifferently set out to take from people. Jesus is talking about a person who couldn't care less about who they injure. *"I'm going to have what I want. And no one is going to stop me."*

I wish I could say I have never met some people like that, but in reality I have: ruthless in the marketplace; vindictive and petty in the neighborhood; and self-serving and demanding at church. Take. Take. Take. That's hypocrisy committed by people still coming to church and singing the songs, raising their hands, and carrying their Bibles. I am always amazed by Christians who can claim to love the Lord but leave a trail of hurting people in their wake and never seem to give a second thought to the damage they have caused.

Let me ask you: Have you injured others and callously turned away? Have you done things knowingly to wound people and then come to church and participated without hesitation? Do your children carry scars from your hypocrisy? Are there people where you work whom you hate? Are there people in your family you hate but you use church as a refuge where you hide from things you haven't dealt with? *That* is hypocrisy. And it cannot exist unchallenged in a New Testament church or the life of an authentic disciple of Jesus.

Notice that hypocrisy is an anchor that will drag your soul into hell if you don't repent of it. Your hypocrisy can lead others astray. Jesus said, **"... You make him twice as much a son of hell as yourselves."**[14] Hypocrisy raises legitimate questions about the reality of your faith. Dealing with personal hypocrisy is an exercise in humility and a step in understanding God's grace. God loves you despite your hypocrisy, but He never wants you to be comfortable with it!

» Habit Three: Squirming my way out of any promise I don't want to keep.
Jesus continued to work through His docket of denunciation against the
Pharisees in Matthew 23:16–22:

> **Woe to you, blind guides, who say, "If anyone swears by the tem-
> ple, it is nothing, but if anyone swears by the gold of the temple,
> he is bound by his oath." You blind fools! For which is greater,
> the gold or the temple that has made the gold sacred? And you
> say, "If anyone swears by the altar, it is nothing, but if anyone
> swears by the gift that is on the altar, he is bound by his oath."
> You blind men! For which is greater, the gift or the altar that
> makes the gift sacred? So whoever swears by the altar swears by
> it and by everything on it. And whoever swears by the temple
> swears by it and by him who dwells in it. And whoever swears by
> heaven swears by the throne of God and by him who sits upon it.**

Here Jesus was describing promise-breaking hypocrisy. *"I say I'll do
something, but then I don't do it. I commit to action, but what I really mean is, 'I'll
make good on my promise if it works out for me.'"* This is probably the number
one disappointment I've felt in almost thirty years of being a pastor; people who say they'll do things and then don't follow through. Hypocritical
excuses are predictable: *"Oh, everything was good for a while, but now, when I
don't get my way; when it's not what I thought; when I'm paying a price personally
to persevere—now I don't like it. My promise is now null and void because what I
really meant in my promise was to take care of myself."*

*"What I really promised was to do what works for me. And when you were
working for me, you were part of my plan. But as soon as you're not working for
me, you're off plan and out of the picture."* These are the statements of those
squirming their way out of promises they don't want to keep. Psalm 15:4
refers to someone **"who swears to his own hurt,"** indicating that the man
or woman of integrity is a person who gives their word and keeps it regardless of the cost. I've made some big personal commitments in my life:

One Savior for life.

One wife for life.

One church for life—if God would allow.

And trust me, those commitments get tested. There are times when it would be a lot easier to go in a different direction. Recognize that if you give your word on something, it will cost you. Ecclesiastes 5:4–5 says, **"When you vow a vow to God, do not delay in paying it, for he has no pleasure in fools. . . . It is better that you should not vow than that you should vow and not pay."** Pay what you vow. Deliver what you promise, or don't promise. That's what sincere, honest people do. Hypocrites, though, squirm out of any promise they don't want to keep.

Matthew 23:16 gives an example of this habit: **"Woe to you, blind guides, who say, 'If anyone swears by the temple, it is nothing, but if anyone swears by the gold of the temple, he is bound by his oath.'"** The word *swears* is not the idea of cursing but of an oath or vow. *Do you swear to tell the truth, the whole truth, and nothing but the truth so help you God?* It's making a solemn promise; giving your word. The Pharisees had a "fingers-crossed-behind-your-back" clause in their commitments. They would say, "I swear by the temple that I'll do this."

And then someone would say, "Hey! You swore by the temple you would do it, but you're not doing it!"

They would respond, "Ah! But I didn't swear by the *gold* in the temple!" They expected to be released from promises based on a hidden technicality. Sound familiar?

Jesus crushes this nonsense and then gives another example: **"You blind fools! For which is greater, the gold or the temple that has made the gold sacred? And you say, 'If anyone swears by the altar, it is nothing . . .'"** (vv. 17–18).

Apparently someone would say, "I promise I'll pay you Thursday. I swear it by the altar."

Then the one who had loaned would say, "Dude, it's Thursday."

And the debtor would say, "Yeah, well, I didn't swear by the *gift* on the altar, so I'm off the hook."

Jesus is coming down hard on hairsplitting. **"You blind men! For which is greater, the gift or the altar that makes the gift sacred? So whoever swears by the altar swears by it and by everything on it"** (vv. 19–20). I mean, we're back in sixth grade here. Jesus was sorting out the nuances of honesty for a bunch of hypocrites.

"And whoever swears by the temple swears by it and by him who dwells in it. And whoever swears by heaven swears by the throne of God and by him who sits upon it" (vv. 21–22). How clear could that be?

Someone said promises are like babies: easy to make and hard to deliver. Do you break your promises to God? Do you say to Him, "I'll tithe; I'll witness; I'll obey," and then look for technicalities to invalidate your commitments? Closer to home, how often do you tell your wife, "I'll do this, honey. I'll get that done; you can count on me" and then you don't do it? It doesn't matter whether it's changing a lightbulb or going on a date. If you say you'll do it, *do it*; keep your word! People who can't count on your word can't trust you.

I was reading a biography of John Lennon and found very tragically in the midst of the story a quote about this famous Beatle. John Lennon's son said, "My dad was a hypocrite. Dad could talk about peace and love out loud to the world. He could sing about it, but he could never show it to the people who supposedly meant the most to him, his wife and his son. How can you talk about peace and love and have a family in bits and pieces, no communication, adultery, divorce? You can't do it; not if you're being true and honest with yourself."[15]

» *Habit Four: Making a big deal of little things and ignoring things of critical importance.*

Jesus continued, **"Woe to you, scribes and Pharisees, hypocrites! For you tithe mint and dill and cumin, and have neglected the weightier matters of the law: justice and mercy and faithfulness. These you ought to have done, without neglecting the others. You blind guides, straining out a gnat and swallowing a camel!"** (vv. 23–24).

Inflating random issues out of size and importance is hypocrisy. Do you tend to obsess over little matters at home or at work? Do you major on minors and minor on majors? Are you out-of-balance in your faith? Some things you are so worked up about and other things, "Pssh. I never think about that. My conscience isn't sensitive at all." Jesus addresses this in verse 23: **"Woe to you, scribes and Pharisees, hypocrites! For you tithe mint and dill and cumin. . . ."** Jesus was mentioning garden herbs that were listed by the Pharisees as subject to the tithe. Tithing is the principle of giving 10 percent of my income off the top to God. In the Old Testament, where everything wasn't currency, a lot of giving involved actual commodities. If you had an apple orchard, you brought a tenth of those apples to the temple for use in worship and to supply the priests. If you had livestock, you contributed a tenth of the increase. A lot of it was giving in kind, but the Bible never prescribed anything in regard to the little garden out behind your house where you raised some herbs for cooking.

Enter the Pharisees. These guys were so spiritual that they didn't hesitate to hold a little sprig of parsley and say, *"One leaf for God; nine leaves for me; one leaf for God; nine leaves for me. I am so godly!"* The Bible never asked for that level of measuring the tithe. But microtithing wasn't the real problem for Jesus. Here was His case: you are so energetic about these little examples, but you ignore the *massive* matters of importance!

We don't have to wonder what Jesus thinks those are. He tells us: **". . . and have neglected the weightier matters of the law: justice and mercy and faithfulness"** (v. 23). He was echoing Micah 6:8, **"He has shown you, O man, what is good; and what does the LORD require of you but to do justly, to love mercy, and to walk humbly with your God?"**[16]

When Christ says *justice*, He's talking about doing what's right. You may well be facing a big decision this week. Do you know what you should do? Let me tell you: don't pray on it anymore—do what's right. "Yeah, but I'm kind of wrestling with the . . ." Do what's right! Right action will always get you to a good place. You will never turn out wrong doing right. And you'll never turn out right doing wrong. Just do the right thing—justice!

And then, notice, Jesus adds *mercy*. Go a little easier on people. "Yeah, well what they're doing is *not right*!" But the Bible says in James 2:13, **"Judgment is without mercy to the one who has shown no mercy."** As I've reviewed a lot of recent interactions, I've looked for times when chances were given, opportunities and time for God to work, time for repentance, and time for reconciliation. Giving others room is very important. I want to show more mercy. **"Mercy triumphs over judgment,"** James 2:13 goes on to say.

And what's Jesus' last concern? Faithfulness. Just keep going. Don't let anything stop you. I'm on it right now: heart, soul, mind, and strength. I am praying and believing that this is going to be my best year spiritually ever . . . ever! I'm praying the same for you as we travel this journey together. We're not going to get sidetracked when life gets difficult sometimes. And I am going to be pushing and driving for that in every chapter as we go through the disciplines of a sincere faith. I'm going to be challenging you to look at your own walk with God—*your* walk with God. If you're reading this and thinking to yourself, "I can't wait to get my sister this book," you've already missed it!

This is for *you*. And these matters are where it has to start: justice, mercy, and faithfulness in your walk with God.

Verse 23 goes on, **"These you ought to have done, without neglecting the others."** Jesus was saying, "You want to tithe your spices? Really?! Knock yourself out. That's fine." It's not the wrong of the micro; it's the absence of the macro. It's claiming to love God in little actions while ignoring Him in what really counts. "Well, I've memorized four Scriptures last week. And I'm reading this good book right now." But do you love people? God is fine with the little things, but don't overlook the big opportunities for obedience!

Jesus adds an unforgettable illustration in verse 24, **"You blind guides, straining out a gnat . . ."** So this is a picture; we're making a nice chicken stew. Our kitchen is in the Middle East, where the windows are open and the bugs visit regularly. And just as it's time to serve the meal, you realize, "Wait! I have discovered a gnat in the soup. I'll have to use a colander to strain it out." And you go to great care to remove the offending insect. Meanwhile, a camel sneaks in the kitchen and dives into the pot—and you don't even notice! This is Christ's picture of hypocrisy: so focused on certain things; so determined to be pure in matter A (gnats); and so completely unplugged from the reality and offense of my impurity in matter B (camels).

"You blind guides, straining out a gnat and swallowing a camel!" (v. 24). Making a big deal of little things and ignoring things of critical importance. We do this in parenting. We do this in our work life. And we make this mistake in our walk with God and in our relationships. It's time for a total hypocrisy makeover—which *won't* happen if we are practicing the next habit.

» *Habit Five: Exhibiting laziness in all matters of the heart.*
"Woe to you, scribes and Pharisees, hypocrites! For you clean the outside of the cup and the plate, but inside they are full of greed and self-indulgence. You blind Pharisee! First clean the inside of the cup and the plate, that the outside also may be clean" (vv. 25–26). In this judgment, Jesus pointed to all matters of the heart—anything having to do with my soul, my faith. He exposed the laziness of hypocrisy in spiritual life—not willing to extend energy in loving God. Can you see the guy Jesus is describing? *"I'm about to take a drink, but before I do, I want to make sure I drink from a beautiful cup. So I'm going to clean up the outside of this mug so it shines."* And though the inside of the cup is filled with stench, you drink it down, delighting in the *appearance* of the container but imbibing the filth it holds.

Jesus doesn't mince words in describing what's inside the beautiful cup: **". . . but inside they are full of greed and self-indulgence"** (v. 25). Notice this very, very bad combination. Greed is, *"I can't get enough;"* self-indulgence is, *"I have no restraint in the consumption of what I have."* The Bible says, **"If riches increase, set not your heart on them."**[17]

Not so long ago, my wife and I had a conversation about a useful object we no longer need. I asked her, "Honey, what should we do with this?"

She said, "We should put it aside and look for someone to give it to."

There's wisdom. But greed says, "I can't have enough. And I have to hold on to everything I have." And self-indulgence says, "I can't be satiated. I will always consume all I have."

Are you someone who always has to have more? Once you have it, must you consume it? *"We're living at the edge. We are existing paycheck to paycheck, and we like it this way. We spend everything we make and a little more all the time—right up to the limits. We could cut back, but we won't."* These are the struggles of someone who is lazy in matters of the heart.

> WE ARE ALL WHO WE ARE WHEN NO ONE CAN SEE US.

If you find yourself identifying with this hypocritical attitude, listen to Jesus' remedy: **"You blind Pharisee! First clean the inside of the cup and the plate, that the outside also may be clean"** (v. 26). This once in the chapter Jesus makes "Pharisee" singular. It's almost as if the laser of His words is seeking out the individual who is vulnerable to the truth and piercing his condition. You blind Pharisee! How can you not see this is wrong? You extend great effort to beautify the exterior while the internal filth is treated with laziness. Too lethargic to work? You steal. Too lazy to discipline yourself? You feed on what you steal without restraint. Not willing to extend the effort for matters unseen. Here's a heart sentence: We are all who we are when no one can see us. When we think someone will see, when others will know, all of us optimize the appearance of what we do. But what do you do when no one is watching and no one will know? That's who you truly are.

But are you satisfied with your condition? Who could hear Jesus' words and not be convicted? You may be thinking, "Why am I having to consider this on Bears' game day (substitute your favorite distraction)? Man! I don't want to think about this kind of stuff right now!" That's hypocritical apathy—exhibiting laziness in matters of the heart. Being stuck and not caring enough to admit it. *"I don't want to do the work!"* What a tragedy to display hypocrisy with Jesus' word "Woe" ringing in your ears.

» *Habit Six: Looking good to others, no matter what the cost.*

This offensive habit takes hypocrisy to a new level. *"I'm going to look good. I'm going to wear and flaunt my façade. I don't care what it costs."* This is a person who is satisfied with their condition. Jesus said, **"Woe to you, scribes and Pharisees, hypocrites! For you are like whitewashed tombs ..."** (v. 27). If you stand on the Mount of Olives in Israel, the valley between you and the city of Jerusalem is a cemetery—a wall-to-wall burial ground. Graves as far as the eye can see. And every year before the Passover, they would clean off the grave covers stained by the weather or dirtied by birds and then whitewash everything. It was said Jerusalem gleamed in the sunlight in the weeks before the festival.

Of course, the fact that the tombs had been whitewashed outside didn't change the insides filled with rotting corpses and dried bones. Jesus' hearers knew the reality behind the picture when He said, **"For you are like whitewashed tombs, which outwardly appear beautiful, but within are full of dead people's bones and all uncleanness. So you also outwardly appear righteous to others, but within you are full of hypocrisy and lawlessness"** (vv. 27–28). He was saying, "Crack your shell, and inside all we'll find is a pattern of you saying one thing and doing the other. And your lack of concern about your spiritual condition will lead to lawlessness." The hypocrite says, *"I don't care what the Bible says. I'm going to do what I want to do."*

At first this might sound a little too obvious to fit us, but, how many times do we come to church looking great, not a hair out of place but missing even a shred of spiritual readiness inside? You would never think of arriving at church with bed-head and wrinkled clothes. Yet how often do we enter worship looking appropriate, but not a moment has been devoted to prayerfully preparing our hearts; no time has been spent in God's Word cultivating a teachable spirit? If we roll in to a worship service fifteen minutes late, thinking that someone should congratulate us for putting ourselves in the seat, we are failing to recognize the God who intends to meet with us. Do we really want to keep the Lord of the universe waiting? What disregard we show! What could be so important any morning that would result in a worship auditorium being half-full of worshipers when the first note of praise was sung? And only full as people came at their own convenience? But looking good! What does external performance with no internal hunger say about our hearts?

"Oh man! For me to get to church on time, do you know how early I would have to get up?" That's the statement you want to make about the way you value the gift of salvation in Christ—you can't get up a little earlier?

What bothers you more, seeing your children misbehave or God seeing *your* disobedience? Arriving at church with your hair out of place or your heart unprepared?

What upsets you most, a spot on your shirt, a stain on your dress, or a lump of repentance in your heart? The habit of contentment with an external shell that misleads others into thinking that all is well on the inside is an attitude God will not leave untroubled. So, are you troubled? How are you doing with the basic questions? *Am I like that? Do I do that?*

» *Habit Seven of Highly Hypocritical People: Pretending to be better than others, no matter what the evidence.*

Jesus ended His list with: **"Woe to you, scribes and Pharisees, hypocrites! For you build the tombs of the prophets and decorate the monuments of the righteous"** (v. 29). The people of Jesus' day had a great heritage featuring the prophets of the Old Testament like Isaiah, Jeremiah, Ezekiel, Daniel, and many more. They would decorate their tombs and hold religious ceremonies at the gravesites of the departed prophets. Jesus did not affirm this practice, whatever its motive. They were behaving more like pagans than biblical believers. But Jesus addresses their hypocritical claim: **"... 'If we had lived in the days of our fathers, we would not have taken part with them in shedding the blood of the prophets'"**

(v. 30). They would stand at the tomb of the murdered prophets and say, "*If we had lived in their day, we would not have done this. We're better than our ancestors.*" Blind! Within days, these people will murder Jesus Christ. They are going to call for His unjust crucifixion. And in their hypocrisy—the Gospels tell us—they will only come to the courtyard of Pilate's house. They won't go *into* Pilate's house because doing so would make them unclean as they approach the Passover. But they'll stand outside and call for the unjust *murder* of Jesus Christ! *Blindness* to their true condition.

"Thus you witness against yourselves that you are sons of those who murdered the prophets" (v. 31). Jesus was making it clear the apple doesn't fall far from the tree. They were just like their fathers.

What follows is one of the hardest statements in all of Christ's teaching: **"Fill up, then, the measure of your fathers"** (v. 32). He's implying here, "You are about to murder Me. Do it! You think you're so much greater than your forefathers? You're about to repeat their mistakes and more!"

"You serpents, you brood of vipers, how are you to escape being sentenced to hell?" (v. 33). A lifetime of unrepentant hypocrisy reveals that a person has never truly been born again. As you read these words, if God's Spirit is provoking conviction in your heart about areas of your life that need to improve or change, those are good signs. There's hope for you! But if all you're thinking about is what *others* need to learn and what a fine Christian you are, those are very bad indications. Jesus' words for you are ominous: **". . . how are you to escape being sentenced to hell? Therefore I send you prophets and wise men and scribes, some of whom you will kill and crucify, and some you will flog in your synagogues and persecute from town to town . . ."** (vv. 33–34). I think of all the pastors and leaders through the years who have been rejected, ridiculed, and run out of town by church people who didn't want to hear the truth. I shake my head in sadness over the price to be paid on a fairly regular basis to stand for what's true regardless of who likes it. I grieve over the punishment exacted on God's servants by those who chose capriciously to refuse the message. Jesus' words still hit their mark today: **". . . so that on you**

may come all the righteous blood shed on earth, from the blood of righteous Abel to the blood of Zechariah the son of Barachiah, whom you murdered . . ." (v. 35). I'm sure they thought, "What!? How does He know about *that*?"

He continues, ". . . between the sanctuary and the altar. Truly, I say to you, all these things will come upon this generation" (vv. 35–36). Within days these men will add more condemnation when they loudly call for Jesus' blood to be on their heads and their children's heads.[18]

The last two words should give us pause—"this generation." Jesus was speaking directly to His audience. But much of what He said applies today. The question is, what would He say to *this* generation about the seven habits of hypocritical people? Are we like that? Do we do that?

CONCLUSION

Let's take a closing look at the Lord's heart in this matter of hypocrisy. Because if you think Jesus Christ is standing over you today, saying, "You hypocrite!" and turning His back on you, you don't understand what was behind even these harsh words from the Lord. If you miss His heart, you lose so much! He goes on to say, "O Jerusalem, Jerusalem, the city that kills the prophets and stones those who are sent to it! How often would I have gathered your children together as a hen gathers her brood under her wings, and you would not!" (v. 37). The offer from heaven flows in these words, alongside the sadness over the many who "will not"! They will hear the invitation and turn away. God will call; they won't answer. Stubbornness of the heart is a terminal sickness. There is no solution for that condition apart from repentance and God's work of grace to break the heart.

And then Jesus says the most ominous words: "See, your house is left to you desolate" (v. 38). You eventually get the spiritual condition your hypocrisy produces. The hypocrite thinks everything is going along fine, but there will be a rude awakening. Others may be fooled; God sees the heart. He sees your intentions, right now. He knows exactly what condition you are in to undertake the rest of this study. I pray as you turn the pages and begin this journey through the disciplines of a sincere faith, you will acknowledge deeply any tendency toward hypocrisy and ask God to prepare you for what He has in store. In fact, pray with me these sincere words recorded by David in Psalm 19:7-14.

The law of the LORD is perfect, reviving the soul; the testimony of the LORD is sure, making wise the simple; the precepts of the LORD are right, rejoicing the heart; the commandment of the LORD is pure, enlightening the eyes; the fear of the LORD is clean, enduring forever; the rules of the LORD are true, and righteous altogether. More to be desired are they than gold, even much fine gold; sweeter also than honey and drippings of the honeycomb. Moreover, by them is your servant warned; in keeping them there is great reward.

Who can discern his errors? Declare me innocent from hidden faults.

Keep back your servant also from presumptuous sins; let them not have dominion over me! Then I shall be blameless, and innocent of great transgression.

Let the words of my mouth and the meditation of my heart be acceptable in your sight, O LORD, my rock and my redeemer.

You have just prayed the *crisis* that lays the foundation for the *process* we will describe in the rest of this book. Believe me, the crisis is crucial. Just ask: *Lord, where am I hypocritical? In what ways am I hypocritical?* And as the Spirit of God pricks your heart about specifics, confess them in that moment. "You're right, Father. You're right and I'm wrong. I want to be authentic. I want to be sincere and genuine with nothing else mixed in. Show me, God, Your true holiness. What do I know of true holiness? Open my heart and mind to You."

Allow me to pray for you as you dedicate yourself to the disciplines of an authentic faith:

Father, I ask You in this moment to grant to this Your child a genuine release from any burden they might have about reading these insights for someone else. Even if they're burdened for someone close to them, release them and give them, by Your Spirit, great freedom to look inside at their own hypocrisy. Help them see how quick they are to judge others, to take up offense, to mount the horse of self-righteousness, demanding of others what they do not demand of themselves. Free us from hypocrisy, Lord, so we may be free to develop the disciplines of an authentic faith. In the strong name of Jesus, I pray, Amen.

THE REAL THING:

On Your Own

FIRST TIMES ARE MEMORABLE moments in living. You can probably say off the top of your head your five favorite "first times" in life, new experiences that came to have special significance. I have a few of my own. Some first times are unforgettable in themselves (like seeing the Grand Canyon or Niagara Falls), and some of them are remarkable because of everything that comes after (like the first time you realize you want *that* woman to be your wife or the first time you discover the joy of playing an instrument). This second kind of experience may not even seem all that significant when it happens, but it grows in importance the longer you live with it. Such is my experience with personal Bible study.

Around the time I was fifteen years old, I was introduced to a tool developed by Jack Wirtzen's Word of Life ministry called a *Quiet Time Journal*. It was a simple method of tracking personal time spent in Bible study throughout the week. Every day's page invited you to ask the same three basic questions about the Bible texts you were reading: What does it say? What does it mean? How does it apply to your life? Thirty-five years later, I'm still asking those same questions when I open the Bible with our congregation each week. My sermons (and much of this book) are composed of repeated sequences of these questions because they are the link between the written Word and the lived Word.

Part of this story has to do with how easily we turn the freedoms offered by a discipline into guilt-ridden hypocrisy driven by legalism. I remember clearly some of the feelings I had after I had been using the *Quiet Time Journal* for a while. In order to keep up the 7/7 pace, I was having to sometimes do three or four "quiet times" a day to catch up for the times I'd missed. Even as I tried to follow the schedule in this way, I knew I was missing the purpose. God never said, "Seven days you shall have a quiet time and you shall not rest from it." Relationships are regular and intimate, but they are not mechanical. A healthy pattern isn't rigid. My wife likes to have a date night each week, but if we miss one, she doesn't hate me. There's much more at stake in my relationship with my wife and my relationship with God than slavishly keeping a calendar. Regularity is one important factor, not the whole picture.

The lessons from my own personal Bible study led me to believe a person who averages five solid times in God's Word each week is a person growing in their faith. The Scriptures don't lay out a definite schedule, so the ones we make for ourselves need to serve the purpose of consistent time with God in His Word. If they become a threat or a discouraging weight, they are not serving their purpose: to facilitate our growing to love our heavenly Father more and more. Ultimately, we want to saturate our minds with God's Word so it can be increasingly said of us, **"his delight is in the law of the Lord, and on his law he meditates day and night. He is like a tree planted by streams of water that yields its fruit in its season, and its leaf does not wither. In all that he does, he prospers."**[1] Please recognize my heart as we delve into these disciplines of a sincere faith. Each of these is intended not to be an intimidating obstacle between you and God but a way of deepening intimacy with the One who has called you His child and wants the best for you.

CHAPTER TWO

THE DISCIPLINE OF PERSONAL BIBLE STUDY

A s I reflect on the chapter you just read, I'm visualizing the response of people when I gave the original message on hypocrisy in a sermon. In one sense the content was so negative and confrontational, and yet I was blown away by the response—openhearted, genuine, and so sincere—in the way people in our congregation received the hard words from Jesus in Matthew 23. It was difficult to teach the passage, but it was literally the honest way into these chapters on authenticity. I'm sure there were plenty of points in the last few pages where personal offense was possible, but here we are, ready to start developing the disciplines of a sincere faith. You and I simply can't appreciate the light until we know what it's like to be in the darkness. We've got to see the problem before we can embrace the solution. But we're ready to embark on a journey toward authenticity.

Now, authentic isn't something you feel first; it's something you do. Do it first; feel it later. We're going to develop the disciplines of a sincere faith. Let's begin in Psalm 19, with verses you used in a prayer in the last chapter. But we're going to visit other places in God's Word too, because the point of this chapter is how we become intimately familiar with the Bible. I want to suggest you need to regularly do three actions in order to develop the discipline of studying God's Word. Here's the first one. You need to . . .

PICK IT UP

"The law of the LORD is perfect, reviving the soul; the testimony of the LORD is sure, making wise the simple; the precepts of the LORD are right, rejoicing the heart; the commandment of the LORD is pure, enlightening the eyes; the fear of the LORD is clean, enduring forever; the rules of the LORD are true, and righteous altogether."[2] Do you know what you are holding when you pick up your Bible? The Bible actually is beyond any other book. No alternative volume is even worthy to be compared to the Word of God. Many people have left eloquent witness to the impact of the Scriptures on their lives and the importance it played in the world. George Washington said, "It is impossible to rightly govern the world without God and the Bible." John Quincy Adams, another American president, said, "So great is my veneration of the Bible that the earlier my children begin to read it, the more confident will be my hope that they will prove useful citizens of their country and respectable members of society."

English author Charles Dickens declared, "The New Testament is the very best book that ever will be known or written in the world."

Andrew Jackson said, "That book, sir, is the Rock upon which our Republic rests."

Abraham Lincoln wrote, "I believe the Bible is the best gift God has ever given to man. All the good from the Savior of the World is communicated to us through this book."

Dwight Eisenhower said, "To read the Bible is to take a trip to a fair land where the spirit is strengthened and renewed."

I've been reading *Decision Points* by George W. Bush. He has many things to say about the importance of God's Word in his life and thinking.

Great people have found their greatness through being affected by God's amazing book.

So the first step in developing a discipline of personal Bible study is to pick it up. While it's exciting to read what people have to say about the Bible, I don't think there's really any better way to appropriately understand what we've picked up and appreciate what we're holding than to look at what God's Word has to say about itself. We're going for firsthand experience.

Psalm 119 is the longest statement in Scripture about the Bible and its value. Almost every one of the 176 verses in the psalm describes something noteworthy about God's Word. You could read one verse a day from this single psalm and go through it twice each year with a few days left over for the ones you miss. A good summary of the main points of Psalm 119 is found in Psalm 19. Starting in verse 7, we have six descriptive titles and six results from Scripture engagement. Here is the first one.

The Bible transforms you.

Psalm 19:7 declares, **"The law of the LORD is perfect, reviving the soul."** God's Word transforms us. It changes me. It renovates you. That's what this verse is saying. In the phrase, **"The law of the LORD,"** the word *law* translates the word *Torah*: law for life; the rule for living. God's Word is the norm. It is the standard by which every other truth is measured or assessed.

Notice the claim of ownership. Scripture is **"The law *of* the LORD."** Through the centuries men have laid down their laws and published their rules. Governments have proposed ways things should be done in society. Yet nations come and nations go, but **"The law of the LORD"** remains.

Next, verse 7 gives a description of God's Word: **"The law of the LORD is *perfect*."** That word *perfect* means literally *all-sided, many faceted, all-encompassing*, and *comprehensive*. **"The law of the LORD"** is so perfect that it revives or (one translation says) it "converts"[3] the soul. Now the soul is the inner, immaterial part of you. I'm sure you realize you're not just a physical person. A part of you is spiritual and will live forever. That's the part of you that can and needs to be converted—your soul. God's Word demonstrates its perfection by transforming you.

I have been blessed to pastor Harvest Bible Chapel through many years, but one of the amazing sights I notice recurs almost every weekend. There is a guy type I have in my mind and when I'm working on my message, I think about this man. I can almost picture where the current version will be sitting. I call this guy Joe Screwdriver. Joe's a regular male, working in his garage, kicking around, trying to make life work. He shows up at Harvest, often at first against his will. Maybe he lost a bet with his wife or he decided to find out what was happening in her life. But he's not sure. And the first week, he sits cross-armed and leaning back—observing. He's here, but in the *I'm not participating* mode. But when weeks become months, I see God's Word transform Joe Screwdriver. First he unfolds his arms; he relaxes. And then he kind of leans forward. At first he projects, *"I'm not singing, dude. I am flat-out not singing. You can't make me. I'm going to show you I don't like what's happening right now."* But we watch him. We observe how God changes the heart of people.

And this is how He does it. Psalm 19:7, **"The law of the LORD is perfect, converting the soul."**[4] God's Word is so powerful it is able to take an unsaved, unregenerated, uninterested, hard-hearted Joe Screwdriver and absolutely turn that guy's life around! Spin him on his head. Raise him up a new person. Arms once folded get lifted and lips once sealed now smile in praise to God.

In what ways can you say, "I'm a different person because of the impact God's Word has made in my life"?

Here's a second effect you can expect from God's Word:

It gives you wisdom.

Psalm 19:7 also says, **"The testimony of the LORD is sure, making wise the simple."** The word *testimony* pictures God as witnessing to Himself. If you want to know what God is like, it's nice to hear from people. But what about God Himself taking the witness stand and saying, "This is what I'm like. This is who I am. This is what I will do for you." The **"testimony of the LORD"** is God bearing witness to Himself. God is not required to tell us about Himself, but He does. If He chose to remain hidden, we wouldn't have a clue, but His love and His plans for us ensure that He lets us know what we need to know. Ultimately, He has spoken through the written Word and His Son, Jesus Christ.[5]

Psalm 19:7 affirms the following about God's self-revelation: **"The testimony of the LORD is sure."** It's dependable and durable. The NIV says it's **"trustworthy."** The word is similar to the term transliterated "amen" in English. We could read this phrase, **"The testimony of the LORD is amen."** It is the real thing; authentic; consistent with God's character. His Word is reliable.

But you're wondering, *"How reliable is the Bible exactly?"*

I'd like to answer that question—right from the source. The testimony of the Lord is so sure, that it **"makes wise the simple"** (v. 7). This is a widely applicable necessity, you see, because Joe Screwdriver's setback is one we all share. We've all been like him. Our problem isn't *just* stubbornness and hard-heartedness. We are also naïve and foolish. The idea behind this word *simple* is actually an *open* or *unguarded mind*. In today's language we would say a simple person has no mental firewalls, virus software, or wise discrimination. The simple person is easily led astray. Their mind is like a house with the front door *and* back doors open. An idea comes in and the simple person thinks, *"That's amazing! I guess that's what I'll believe."* But then another thought blows in and they switch mental gears: *"I'm going to follow this guy now. He's the latest author featured on all the talk shows. I was just at Barnes & Noble and picked up his bestselling how-to-fix-my-life book. I hope it will finally do it for me."* This simple person can't hang on to what matters because they don't have the capacity to feel the weight of what is substantive or notice the influence of what is light, fluffy, and foolish. They have no discernment. The world may have high praise for the so-called open-minded person, but godly wisdom controls access to the mind. G. K. Chesterton said, "The problem with a lot of open minds is that they need to be closed down for repairs!"

Now *that* is a big problem. And we have all been that open, deer-in-the-headlights kind of simple person. But the testimonies of the Lord are so sure that they can make a foolish, vacillating, undiscerning person into a wise person. My friend Joe Screwdriver? He used to be an easy mark for the world—but he's so wise now. The things he says, the insights he has, and the understanding he brings to conversations are remarkable. *"Where did this come from?"* We know where it came from. God's Word is pouring wisdom into Joe's life just like it can pour into yours and mine.

Here's the third expectation God's Word delivers, from the beginning of verse 8.

It brings you joy.

"The precepts of the LORD are right, rejoicing the heart."[6] God's Word brings joy to our hearts. I don't think when I'm preparing a sermon, *"What should I say about the Bible?"* No, we look into the Word to hear what God says about the book He has given us. And here He begins, **"The precepts of the LORD are right..."** The idea behind *statutes* or *precepts* relates to the concept of *divine principles; God's rulings, prescriptions, and pronouncements; God's charges.* The world has a lot of precepts or principles. Worldly wisdom says, "You only go around once"; "You've got to go for all you can get"; or even a perennial favorite like, "Fool me once, shame on you; fool me twice, shame on me." Now cronies may revel in all these kind of, honestly, "stupidisms," yet they are really nonsense. When you put those sayings alongside God's Word? No comparison!

Here's the bottom line: God's **"precepts"** are right. Who's right? God is the one who is right. There is no discussion. The latest atheistic tripe is incorrect. Unless the atheists have decided to agree with God, God is right and they are wrong. God is not only good all the time; He's also right all the time. His precepts are a phenomenal thing to have in your hands and mind. But the best part of this is they are so right, they rejoice your heart.

The joy that comes from God's Word summarizes my own life. I was a stupid, foolish, pot-smoking, rebellious teenager. The first big change in me came when I gave the Bible a chance. And God's Word gave me a joy like I had never experienced before. Reading the Bible allowed me to join the disciples as they walked with Jesus on the road to Emmaus. As the Bible describes that journey, **"He interpreted to them in all the Scriptures the things concerning himself."**[7] And later, when they suddenly recognized Him in the breaking of the bread and He left them, they said: **"Did not our hearts burn within us while he talked with us on the road, while he opened to us the Scriptures?"**[8] Sometimes joy feels like a slow burn inside that makes you realize God's Word has brought you close to God Himself.

The character of God's Word explains how I got to be in training for ministry and then helped plant Harvest Bible Chapel. Behind all that was going on, there were the **"statutes of the LORD,"** continually right, rejoicing the heart. God was stirring a joy within me by His Word—something I had never really experienced before.

God's Word transforms us; it gives us wisdom and it brings us joy. But there is more. Here is a fourth result from exposure to the Bible:

It dispels the darkness.

"The commandment of the LORD is pure, enlightening the eyes."[9] Obviously, part of God's Word is commands. Now I'm fine with God telling me certain things. I trust Him. God's Word is filled with, "Do this and you will be blessed; do that and you will suffer." We always say, *choose to sin; choose to suffer.* Every time God says, "Don't," He means, "Don't hurt yourself." I've said that so many times, I hear the echo even when I'm not saying it.

Actually, I wish that word **"pure"** had been translated *clear.* That's the intent of the term—clarity. It's not cloudy or uncertain. God's Word is transparently obvious.

A lot of people have the sense that the Bible is a puzzle. I have a thing with puzzles. These little contraptions with metal parts all knotted up that can be separated—at least that's what they advertise. Each Christmas, the family knows that I am predictable. I usually get a little puzzle among my gifts and I could easily spend hours in a corner, working on my new toy instead of enjoying the family. So they told me, "Here's your box, Dad. We know and you know what's inside. Do not open this present." So I didn't. And we had a great time together. Then afterward, I had to get into those puzzles. But I haven't solved one of them yet!

But the Bible is not a puzzle. It's clear. You can understand it. It yields its message to the normal, attentive person. Be done with people who have put the Bible on such a high shelf you feel like you can't get to it. There's not one person reading this book who isn't in a position to understand the Bible. *You* can grasp it. *You* can comprehend it, be blessed by it, and be changed by it. **"The commandment of the LORD is** (let's say) **clear, enlightening the eyes."**

I could fill volumes of testimonies from people who would be delighted to rise and declare, "I used to see life as a random mess, but now because of the Bible, I see God's design." "I used to think about marriage the world's way, but then God's Word intervened and my mind has been enlightened." "I used to think about parenting one way and then the Bible clarified my thoughts about spanking, disciplining, and really loving my kids." We all start with *our* ideas about something, but we need to learn to submit those thoughts to God's Word—it's so clear. I speak from personal experience: the commands of the Lord, they enlightened my eyes. The Bible dispelled my darkness.

How often in this past week or month have you been aware of darkness in you? You've lain awake, tossing and turning. Or you've puzzled, fretted, worried, and paced about something up ahead. "It's coming. I don't know what it is." God's Word is the light He has given to dispel darkness in you. Pick it up! Before you can rightly utilize God's Word, you must have it in your hands.

When you do, you will discover everything we've already covered and more. Here is a fifth result from regular exposure to the Word of God.

It adds stability.

Psalm 19:9 reminds us, **"The fear of the LORD is clean, enduring forever."** The response called the **"fear of the LORD"** is just that: it's the fear of God. Don't let anybody tell you it's simply *respect* for God. Our response *becomes* respect, but real awareness

> THE FEAR OF LORD IS THE ATTITUDE OF HEART THAT SEEKS TO BE IN A RIGHT RELATIONSHIP WITH THE FEAR SOURCE.

of God starts off as *fear*. The fear of Lord is the attitude of a heart seeking to be in a right relationship with the fear source.

You say, "Well, James, are *you* afraid of God?"

Definitely! At the core I am afraid if I make a wrong decision, God won't hesitate to let me experience consequences. **"God is not mocked, for whatever (I) one sows, that will (I) he also reap."**[10] You will, too. And I'm fearful of being on the wrong side of God. In Psalm 19:9, God's Word is being called **"the fear of the LORD"** because regular exposure to God's Word generates a deepening understanding of who God is—which in turn heightens healthy fear of God.

Do you remember the two thieves on crosses with Jesus described in Luke 23? One said, **"Remember me when you come into your kingdom"** (v. 42). And Jesus responded, **"Today you will be with me in Paradise"** (v. 43). The other guy was—and it's hard to believe—witnessing the Son of God being crucified right beside him. But he mockingly says, "If You are really God, why don't You get us down off these crosses?" (v. 39). The repentant thief was so offended by the disrespectful one that he said, **"Do you not fear God, since you are under the same sentence of condemnation? And we indeed justly, for we are receiving the due reward of our deeds; but this man has done nothing wrong"** (vv. 40–41). One thief had a true sense of who God was and his own condition as a sinner. He wanted to be in a right relationship with God and realized Jesus was his only hope. That's the fear of the Lord.

Psalm 19:9 says that the fear of the Lord is **"clean,"** meaning *without blemish, undiminished, consistently uncompromised, without dilution or* *defilement.* It's full strength! It's not watered down. It's pure. As a result, it endures forever. God's Word is a source of stability when circumstances shake our world. In every place, in every generation, throughout every century, the Bible has been an ever-present help to all who turn to it. God's Word can be that powerful stabilizing component in your life.

And last—here is a sixth expectation from God's Word:

It promises justice.

"The rules of the LORD are true, and altogether righteous."[11] *Rules* means *the rulings* or *declarations.* One translation says, **"judgments of the LORD."**[12] These are God's verdicts, His pronouncements and decisive actions. Man chooses wrong; God administers consequences and ultimately judgment. Man turns from sin, repents and believes; and God dispenses grace. These are the true judgments of the Lord: Do A—get this result . . . always. Do B—get that result . . . always.

The point here is: God's Word promises justice. I don't know about you, but one of the things I find hardest to manage is my heart's longing for justice. If I see something wrong, I want to make it right. If I witness somebody doing something they shouldn't do, I find myself praying, "Make it right, God." When I read the paper or watch the news and I hear about rape, murder, or kidnapping, I cry to God for justice. I was reading this morning about an abortion doctor who had, since 1993, been a known murderer of full-term babies. He regularly birthed children live and then killed them! I want that *fixed*! I want it stopped.

If you know what it is to have a longing in your heart for justice, you need to understand that God's Word makes certain pronouncements: what God thinks about everything that happens; what He will do about all of it. This is the Word of God. **"The judgments of the LORD are true."** He will make things right. Sin *will* be stopped—permanently.

But part of the problem right now is what usually happens when Criminal X or Bad Person Y goes to court. Even when found guilty, he probably won't get what he deserves. Court proceedings are often a reflection of how deep the pockets are of the accused rather than the service of justice. And shockingly, people who are clearly at fault often escape punishment on legal technicalities. But human justice is not the final Court of Appeal. There's no statute of limitations with God when it comes to sin. In the end, God will balance the books of justice. **"The judgments of the LORD are true"** is the declaration of His intent. This affirmation should comfort our hearts when we hunger and thirst for righteousness. Jesus promised[13] we will be satisfied. Meanwhile, we should leave matters of vengeance with the Lord.

All the above to say this: pick it up. Get God's Word in your hands. O that I could be God's Holy Spirit to you, convincing you to engage His book.

With this challenge before us, I know we need to talk about why some of you who are reading this will *not* open God's Word. Picture in your mind the old *Family Feud* game show format on TV. We surveyed 100 people and the top four answers are on the board to this question: Describe a reason people give for not picking up the Bible.

4   NOT INTERESTING

3   XXXXXXXXXXXXXXXXXX

2   XXXXXXXXXXXXXXXXXX

1   XXXXXXXXXXXXXXXXXX

Now that's clearly a statement from someone who doesn't know what they're talking about. *And how many times have you actually been "in" the Bible to reach that finding?*

"Well, one time I read it in fourth grade . . . it didn't have enough pictures."

"I have a friend who told me he knew someone who read the Bible and reported conclusively it's not very engaging or interesting."

Yeah? You need to give God's book another look. Or maybe you need to be honest enough to admit your attitude toward the Bible is completely an impression from others. It's time not to be the person anymore whose exposure to God is all secondhand. You can read the book God meant for *you* to read. When your heart is right and ready, you will find God's Word gripping.

Here's the third most often-given reason for not reading the Bible:

4   NOT INTERESTING

3   I FORGET

2   XXXXXXXXXXXXXXXXX

1   XXXXXXXXXXXXXXXXX

I think answer three is a little more legit. "I get up; I get busy; the Bible gets postponed." How many times in the last month have you intended to get into the Word and got onto your computer instead? How often have you planned to open Scripture but instead poured your cup of coffee or were pulled to some task around the house? How many of us think about reading the Bible but instead can't resist checking our phone to see if we got a text message? And before we know it, it's noon and God's Word is still untouched.

We understand intent doesn't always become reality. We have to admit when our reasons for not getting into God's Word are simply, "I forget. I get off-track." Just remember that *explanation* is not *excuse*. Realizing what we do doesn't let us off the hook; it confronts us with the need to make a different plan than the one we're using—because it's not working.

Here's the second most-given reason for not engaging in regular Bible reading:

4   NOT INTERESTING

3   I FORGET

2   I DON'T UNDERSTAND IT

1   XXXXXXXXXXXXXXXXX

There was a time when unfamiliarity seemed like lack of understanding to me, also. It *looked* thick and complicated so I assumed I wouldn't understand it! People genuinely feel that way, and they unfortunately accept inexperience as the permanent obstacle between them and God's Word. That definitely doesn't have to be the case. I'm going to address lack of exposure a little bit later in this chapter.

And lastly, the most-frequent reason people gave for irregular Bible reading was:

4 NOT INTERESTING
3 I FORGET
2 I DON'T UNDERSTAND IT
1 TOO BUSY

Not great. And not a legitimate answer. It's not even a *real* answer—just a lame excuse. We are *not* too busy to do what really matters. If it's important to us, we get to it. So if we're *too busy* to get into God's Word, then clearly we are—*too busy*. But we're going to conquer some of these obstacles as we develop the disciplines of a sincere faith.

Here's the second of the three actions you need to regularly do in order to improve the discipline of God's Word. First, you have to pick it up. And second, you have to . . .

SIZE IT UP

You've got to actually know what you're holding in your hands to be able to appreciate it. Let's take a step beyond unfamiliarity. Are you willing to wade into the Bible with me in the next few pages and let it argue for its own validity? In order to help you do that, we're going to look at some Bible passages that I'm going to include here, but I urge you to look them up in your Bible. Get used to the open pages I trust will become an intimate place where you meet God. Each verse will describe a certain effect or work God's Word can produce in our lives.

God's Word is fire.

In Jeremiah 5:14 God tells His prophet, **"Behold, I am making my words in your mouth a fire, and this people wood, and the fire shall consume them."** The book God gave us is—fire. God's Word is hot! It is aggressive! The message is purifying. It is not to be trifled with. Scripture consumes all of the obstacles in its path. It burns away the dross and what is useless.

I can't tell you how often I have gotten into God's Word with my mind in a muddle: straw, cobwebs, and dust. But God's Word vaporizes the nonsense in my thinking and gets me on subject and on task. That's the idea of God's Word as a consuming and cleansing fire—like God Himself.

God's Word is a sword.

Here's the second effect of the Bible. Hebrews 4:12 says: **"For the word of God is living and active, sharper than any two-edged sword, piercing to the division of soul and of spirit, of joints and of marrow, and discerning the thoughts and intentions of the heart."** God's Word is a *sword*.

As kids, church activities included what were called Sword Drills. The term comes from this verse. You had to raise your Bible, holding it by the spine. The group was given a reference, like John 3:16. When the command "Charge!" was shouted, the covers flew open and the pages started flipping. We practiced for hours finding verses in our Bibles. The first kid would stand up, and yell, "I've got it! I've got it!" Mastery of the sword resulted in little rewards and encouragement. I can remember my mom having us handle the Scriptures often in Bible club, and this simple drill taught us to find our way inside God's Word. Why not make this kind of Bible exercise part of your family life, where not just the kids but everyone at the table has to wield their copy of the Scriptures?

Here's the point of the story (not Sword Drills): Hebrews 4:12 says the Bible is something **"... living and active, sharper than any two-edged sword, penetrating** (or dividing) **the joints and of marrow."** Like a scalpel, God's Word cuts right to the heart of the matter when we let it speak into our lives.

Too often we discuss things in our homes, in the marketplace, or in our small group and before long we're off on tangents that distract us from what God wants us to realize. The Word of God gets to the truth. Those who are careless about matters of the heart discover God's Word can have a shocking and severing effect. It separates what shouldn't be from what should be. The surgical precision of God's Word is a wonderful gift He has given to us.

God's Word is a hammer.

Back to Jeremiah for another description of the effects of the Bible. In Jeremiah 23:29, God adds a further characteristic of His Word: **"Is not my word like fire** (we've seen that already), **declares the LORD,** (but here's another thing) **and like a hammer that breaks the rock in pieces?"** God's Word is like a maul. Have you ever experienced the hammering impact of God's Word? I needed it. I was so stubborn. It took the persistent blows of the God's Word striking my life, cracking and shaping it to start forming Christ in me. I'm among many who have had to say after a hard episode with Scripture, "God broke a hard rock tonight." This verse gave rise to one of the sayings heard frequently around Harvest: Don't get between the hammer and the work! Letting ourselves and others be exposed to the power of God's Word is a spiritual discipline.

> **DON'T GET BETWEEN THE HAMMER AND THE WORK!**

Maybe you're reading along right now and realize your heart has become hard. Your attitude has become flat-out resistant to God. I know there's nothing clever I can write that will break through the hardness. But give God's Word a chance.

You say, "But I'm so stubborn!"

Open God's Word. It is the hammer able to break the rock in pieces. Are you ready to let God's Word do its work in your life?

God's Word is a seed.

Let's turn to 1 Peter 1:23 for another picture of the work of God's Word: **"...you have been born again, not of perishable seed but of imperishable, through the living and abiding Word of God."** Jesus told several parables about the Word of God being a seed.[14] Later, Peter simply applied Jesus' message under the inspiration of the Holy Spirit—the Word of God is a seed.

Now when we say the Word of God is seedlike, we mean the discipline of "planting" Scripture in the soil of your mind will yield results as surely as depositing a fertile seed in the ground. A farmer's task of planting may not seem all that exciting, but when the living shoots begin to appear across the landscape, who isn't just a little thrilled and amazed? The truths in God's Word have satisfied the greatest minds in human history. They have discovered we're not even capable of framing questions that the Bible doesn't answer. It is so far beyond us. The most persistent students of Scripture know they haven't begun to plumb the depths of God's Word. That's why it's called a seed. It appears small, but it contains the seedlike power and potential to multiply, grow, and bear fruit. God's Word can create the same results.

God's Word is milk.

The apostle Peter gives us another helpful picture of Scripture in his first letter: **"Like newborn infants, long for the pure spiritual milk, that by it you may grow up into salvation"** (2:2). I have recently experienced some significant changes in my life I find difficult not mentioning—I'm now a grandfather. I'm obviously pretty fired up about these grandkids. I had forgotten that not for days, not for weeks but for months babies eat nothing but milk. Really?! A milk only diet? I keep saying to my daughter, Abby, "When are you going to give that kid some food?"

"Not yet, Dad. Not yet."

"Man, that's harsh! Give the child some meat, girl."

"Not yet."

Milk is all they need. The Word of God prescribes the same sequence in our exposure to the Scriptures. For a time in our spiritual lives, we are babies. That's why Peter can say, **"Like newborn infants . . ."** If conversion is like birth, then it makes sense to call the first period of life after salvation "spiritual infancy." During a recent year almost a thousand adults were baptized in our church. Like them, if you're a babe in Christ, a young believer, you need the Word of God like a baby needs milk. You require it desperately and consistently. You ought to wake up and cry for the Scriptures. Not once a day but several times a day. And you ought to be calling out, longing, and looking for it. Just like a baby's body needs milk, so a new Christian's soul needs the Word of God.

We've now sized up the Bible in five ways, seeing it as a fire, a sword, a hammer, a seed, and milk. We're looking at the Scriptures from different angles. And we're asking the question: I've picked it up. Now I'm sizing it up. What is it exactly that God has given to me?

But we're not done looking. Hebrews gives us a further significant picture of God's Word beyond milk.

God's Word is meat.

Hebrews 5:12–13 begins, **"For though by this time you ought to be teachers, you need someone to teach you again the basic principles of the oracles of God. You need milk, not solid food** (or meat)**, for everyone who lives on milk ..."** Unfortunately, some Christians never graduate to the solid food—the meat—of the Bible. Now when the verse says *meat*, it's not describing God's Word as raw or unprepared. The Scriptures are God's gourmet feast! And eating lots of it has none of the unhealthy side effects we experience after eating too much of the daily bread. God's Word is satisfying and nourishing.

I grieve for Christians who are of spiritual school-age, junior high, or high school chronologically but they are still eating the diet of a baby. They appear grown up but are still living on milk like our little grand-babies. You may need to address your spiritual health by chewing and consuming more of the meat in God's Word.

God's Word is light.

"Your word is a lamp to my feet and a light to my path."[15] Many of us have found ourselves standing over milk that's been spilt, plans that went south, and bad decisions that were made—and we know *why* our choices didn't work out. They failed because we made them in the darkness. We didn't consult God's Word. We didn't get the counsel of the Lord through the Lord's people and the Word of God. Or we did, but didn't trust the guidance we received. So we made a bad decision. And we experienced the consequences.

The Bible is a lamp to our feet. "Lamp" means I'm walking in the dark world and God's Word shows me where to step. But it also shines on my path ahead like a flashlight. Not just the next step but where I am going with my life. What is my life to be all about? Where will I end up? What matters the most? God's Word is a lamp to my walking, a light to my journey. No more wandering and stumbling down dead ends and getting ripped off. God's Word helps me walk and live in the light.

Which brings us to the last aspect of the Bible that develops naturally once we are living in its light. We not only can see what's out ahead; we can also see ourselves like never before.

God's Word is a mirror.

"For if anyone is a hearer of the word and not a doer, he is like a man who looks intently at his natural face in a mirror. For he looks at himself and goes away and at once forgets what he was like. But the one who looks into the perfect law, the law of liberty, and perseveres, being no hearer who forgets but a doer who acts, he will be blessed in his doing."[16] God's Word is a mirror. If you only come to church and hear what the Word says, you're like a person who looks at a mirror and goes, *"You know what I just noticed? I have some mustard on my face. I should probably wipe that off. And I will . . . tomorrow."* The response reveals a foolish person. They are a hearer of the Word who is unwilling to be a doer. The person who allows God's Word to be truly a mirror is someone who expects God to reveal who they really are. And then they act upon what He says.

James continues, **"But the one who looks into the perfect law, the law of liberty, and perseveres, being no hearer who forgets but a doer who acts, he will be blessed in his doing."**[17] The Bible warns, but it also and more often offers great reward for those who will take God at His Word. This verse indicates that God wants to bless us *because* we are doing His Word but also *"in"* our doing of His Word. There's something deeply satisfying about seeing the commands and guidance in the Bible and immediately putting them into action. This is why we must add a crucial third decision to the two major actions regarding God's Word that we've already examined (Pick it up; Size it up):

EAT IT UP

Jeremiah 15:16 declares, **"Your words were found, and I ate them, and your words became to me a joy and the delight of my heart, for I am called by your name, O LORD, God of hosts."** We must consume God's Word. It's not enough to hold it. "I carry my Bible everywhere I go. I have one in my purse and on my phone. I even have one in my glove compartment."

It's not enough to even size it up. "I respect it. I revere the Word of God. I value the Bible and can witness to its life-changing power."

You have to *ingest* it yourself. You have to hide His Word in your heart that you might not sin against God.[18] Jeremiah 15:16 is my life verse; a passage in Scripture that resonates with the way God made me. It never ceases to remind me of all He has done and is doing for me. **"Your words were found** (to me, a nineteen-year-old stubborn, rebellious student)**, and I ate them, and your words became to me a joy and the delight of my heart."** In ways I could not anticipate until I took God at His Word, the Scriptures have become the nourishment and delight in my life to affect me in the best ways every day.

So what do I mean by "eat it up"? How does God's Word function as the bread of life and spiritual meat for me? A good meal of Bible feasting includes at least five basic "courses" to ensure healthy and satisfying spiritual nourishment:

Read it.

First of all, this is fairly straightforward: *read* the Bible. Read it out loud, silently, or listen to it read (try all these ways). Be attentive, alert, and thoughtful. As you read, practice doing what you do as you enjoy a great meal, lovingly prepared. Thank God as you savor unexpected "flavors" from the book He has prepared for you.

The Bible is lot like a textbook in the sense that you've got to start in the right places. But unlike a textbook, it doesn't have the easiest stuff at the beginning and the hardest stuff at the end. There is a lot in the Bible that is 2+2=4. And there is a lot in the Bible that's algebra. You say, "Algebra's no problem." But you've got to brush up on basic math before you can get to algebra. Bible reading is a skill every one of us can continually improve.

So let me tell you where some simple (yet profound) equations are in the Bible. For sure, remember two of John's contributions: the gospel of John and 1 John. Those are easily understood, accessible to anyone, parts of Scripture. Now ease doesn't mean these books are one-and-done reads. You will readily comprehend John's gospel, but you will also find yourself returning to its depths throughout your life. The parts of God's Word with which we are most familiar have an uncanny way of appearing new to us when the Holy Spirit applies them to our lives again in unexpected ways.

But when it comes to your early days of intentional Bible reading, don't jump into Ecclesiastes, Song of Solomon, or the Major Prophets of the Old Testament. They are at the deep end of the pool. Hebrews in the New Testament will become much clearer to you once you have the story and flow of the Old Testament under your belt. You can get there. Growth in biblical literacy is attainable for everyone.

Recently I have returned again to the gospel of John. Why don't you join me? Read it. I would suggest this: a chapter a day; not three verses, or three hundred verses. I know that a lot of people like to read through the Bible in a year. That's great! But I'm trying to get more people on board the Bible Train. So aim for a chapter a day. No guilt about anything other than just a chapter a day.

Open with a brief word of prayer. I sit in a chair. I lean forward. I don't read the Bible lying down. I don't know about you, but when I lie down I pass out. So I put my Bible on my desk. I have a pen in my hand and a journal near so I have a place to write thoughts. Because the second practice you want to develop is:

Question it.

You've got to question the Bible. I don't mean object to it; I mean read with an inquisitive attitude. Some of your questions will be directed to the text: who's involved here, what's the big picture around this passage, where else in Scripture are these matters discussed? Many of the questions need to be more personal. Here are a few crucial ones: "Is there an example here for me to follow? Is Jesus doing something I should be doing? Is Herod doing something I *shouldn't* be doing?" It could be a positive or negative example. Questioning the Bible should lead to application insights for you.

Be open to the Bible's convicting work. "Is there a sin for me to confess?" God's Word will expose and confront you. "Is there something here I need to acknowledge or for which I need to repent? Lord, I'm like *that*. I'm wrong, God." And just right there, confess it to Him.

Be teachable. "Is there a truth for me to understand?" Sometimes God just wants to expand our thinking. "I didn't know that about God. He's so tender. He is so loving. He's so forgiving, insistent, pursuing, and truthful. Is there a truth for me to embrace in a deeper way?"

And then last: "Is there a comfort for me to experience? Is God's Word assuring me about something? I can be anxious, fearful, uncertain, and vacillating. Is there an encouraging word I need?" All these questions should be scrolling in the background of your mind as you read the Bible.

But if you really want to get to where the Bible takes you, you've got to go to this next level, and most people do not.

Plan it.

Read it, question it, and then create a plan of action. Pull the journal over and make some notes. Record decisions and discoveries you just made. Date them. If God's Word says something about **"wrath stirs up strife . . .,"**[19] note what changes that truth is going to require of you. A week ago I had to acknowledge to a couple of my staff members, "I was angry with you. And I'm sorry for my reaction. Please forgive me." Conviction and the decision to apologize began as a result of my own time with the Lord. Because when God's Word convicts you, you have to make a plan to do something about the matter—not just to agree with it. So create a plan with a goal and a time. Say, *I'm going to take some action in this regard.*

Pray it.

These last steps have really helped me. I always have my prayer time as part of my Bible reading. When God has been speaking to me, my first response needs to be to Him (more about prayer in the next chapter). The first part of my prayer time after worship is, "Thank You, Lord, for speaking to me from Your Word today. Thank You, Father, for challenging me about this. I agree with Your Word when it says . . ." And pray about your plan of action.

Share it.

I don't do this every day, but I'll frequently say to my wife or to my grown children, "I got this out of the Word today. I've been studying that passage, and this is what it has meant to me." It helps me internalize and apply what God says to me when I put it into words for others. So I'll just take someone aside and say, "Andy, look what I got out of God's Word today. And here is how I'm applying it. What do you think about this?" Or, "Isn't this a great verse?" Share with people you come in contact with. "I found this amazing idea in the Bible." I've been doing that for over thirty years and I'm not lacking for content. Thoughts are always alive and fresh from God's living Word.

Let's use Scripture to **"stir up one another to love and good works!"**[20]

CONCLUSION

Colossians 3:15 begins, **"Let the peace of Christ . . ."** When we read the verse with our question screen up and running, we're asking, "Do I have the peace of Christ? Is there an example of Christ's peace for me to follow? Is there a sin, an anxiety, the opposite of peace for me to confess?" Sometimes my heart is like a tornado and my friends are like an added wind. I need to **"Let the peace of Christ rule in** (my) **heart"**—not other people; not circumstances. I need Jesus to speak peace into my emotions and mind. I don't want to overlook the fact that I've been **"called"** (v. 15) to live in peace with others in the body of Christ. And I need to be **"thankful"** (v. 15). Gratitude should naturally flow when we realize the source of our peace. When Christ is ruling my heart, I'm thankful even when I'm not feeling peace at that moment. The reality of Christ's peace is larger than my feelings.

And I need to let **"the Word of Christ dwell in** (me) **richly"** (v. 16). How many of us are wealthy in a human sense and even well off in a relational sense, but remain penniless in regard to God's Word. I'm going to let the Word of Christ dwell in me richly. I'm not only going to treat it as something of supreme value, I'm also going to saturate my life with it until the valuable by-products of God's Word become apparent in me.

In all of the above my intention has been to introduce you to the discipline of the authentic Christian life that involves regular input from God's Word. I couldn't be more excited about the real possibility that a number of people will take this significant step. Will you get into God's Word this week? Will you dig into it afresh? You and I are not authentic Christians unless we are intentionally, regularly connected to the Word of God. We begin to demonstrate the effects of authenticity when we develop the discipline of God's Word. It is one of the nonnegotiable components of a sincere faith.

Allow me to close this chapter in the way I close each of my times in God's Word—with a prayer for you:

Father, thank You for this great privilege You have given us who call upon Your name to dig into Your Word. We would confess in this moment, Lord, too often we have neglected the book You gave us. Too often we have fattened our souls on things that don't satisfy. And the hunger we feel, the aching inside is a longing You've placed there by Your Spirit for Your Word.

Help us, God, to take it in our hands. Pursue us by Your Spirit this week. Every morning when we wake up, stir the desire within us, God, to pick this book up, to size

THE REAL THING:

Talking with God

THE BIGGEST BREAKTHROUGH I've ever had in my life regarding prayer
came through reading a book while I was at Tennessee Temple University,
just out of high school and very far from home. In that time of loneliness, I
realized I needed to learn how to spend time with God in prayer. The book
was entitled *Discovering How to Pray* by Hope MacDonald (I'd love to claim
her as a long-lost aunt, but she's no direct relation). She included a number
of insights about prayer I had never been taught before. These were simple
but profound suggestions that came at just the right time for me.

One very helpful section of the book was a discussion on posture in
prayer. Until that time I had never knelt down to pray. I can still vividly
remember some of the places on the university campus where I felt led
to kneel in prayer. She also talked about praying out loud as a deliberate choice, even when we are alone. I had never prayed audibly in private
prayer—I was always thinking what I hoped were prayerful thoughts to
God but I had never heard my own voice in private conversation with
God. Had I been asked at the time, I probably would have said that since
God spoke to me through His Word in an inaudible voice, it had seemed
natural to respond the same way. When I began to practice this discipline
of praying out loud, I realized it focused my thoughts and helped me resist

meandering prayer times. Kneeling and speaking to God revolutionized my prayer practice and made the times with Him significantly more intimate. I was no longer thinking off the cuff, on the run, fending off other intruding thoughts. I was on my knees, before my Father, doing my best to put my thoughts into words in His presence.

But the most effective concept this author described had to do with the content and assumptions of my prayers. She encouraged her readers to visualize their prayers already answered as they were being verbalized. If you are praying for a prodigal child, picture the event you are praying for—"Lord, I can see him returning to You. I see him standing beside me in church, singing Your praises, delighted to be in Your presence. I can picture him sitting in his room reading Your Word and letting what You are teaching him filter into his conversations with me so I know You're renewing his mind." Visualizing the prayer fulfilled and saying, "I believe that's going to happen, Lord."

Decades later I can think of the many crises I have lifted to God in prayer, including serious health challenges, ministry catastrophes, and wandering children, and I know this aspect of the discipline of prayer has been consistently beneficial to me. I picture the prayer as answered. I express it as vividly and clearly to God as I'm able, believing it's part of the future He has in store for me. No, I'm not trying to dictate to God how He should answer, but I've found that lurking behind some of our hesitation to picture our prayers as answered is the fear that God *won't* answer. The willingness to vividly imagine what God's answer *could* look like is a much more definite statement of faith than half-letting-Him-off-the-hook by saying, "I believe You can do something about this—whatever." Are we really afraid God can't deliver what we can imagine? What did Paul mean when he wrote, **"Now to him who is able to do far more abundantly than all that we ask or think, according to the power at work within us . . ."**[1] Or as our forefathers put it, **". . . unto him that is able to do *exceedingly abundantly* above all that we ask or think!"**[2] Are those words just doxological hyperbole, or do they express an absolute truth we can put into practice when we pray? I've found when I see my prayer answered, God delights in proving me *not* bold or vivid enough! He does far more than I ask or think. And the biggest surprises aren't just the way He answers prayer but the way He changes me.

CHAPTER THREE

THE DISCIPLINE OF PERSONAL PRAYER

Some 90 percent of Americans claim they pray weekly. Seventy percent say they pray at least daily. It would appear all kinds of praying is going on . . . and yet there also seems to be evidence that what we call prayer doesn't really fit with what God expects from us. Dig under people's reports about praying a lot and you discover they are going through the motions, treating prayer the same way they approach rolling a dice. They're frustrated about prayer even as they try to practice it. They often mention prayer without actually addressing God. And when they do voice their prayers, they are talking to someone they don't even know. God is the complete stranger on the street they might ask for help if things get bad enough.

As we develop the core disciplines of a sincere faith, we must include work on prayer. Even those of us who have grown up around praying people need instruction. And who better to talk to us about prayer than Jesus Christ. That's what we find Him doing in Matthew 6.

The twelve original disciples spent three years hanging out with Jesus. They watched Him, traveled with Him, and listened to Him. There is no record they ever asked Him, "Lord, teach us to teach," even though He was a Master Teacher. Not once did they say, "Lord, teach us how to do miracles," though we know He worked awesome wonders. As far as we know, the only request like this the disciples ever made to Jesus was, **"Lord, teach us to pray."**[3]

They had a front row seat to all that Jesus Christ was and His prayer life really caught their attention. John summarizes their experience in a powerful way: **"And the Word became flesh and dwelt among us, and we have seen his glory, glory as of the only Son from the Father, full of grace and truth."**[4] The disciples were exposed to Jesus 24/7 and their conclusion was, "The thing we've got to figure out is the prayer thing. Jesus has that *going on!*"

Not surprising of the second person of the Trinity, eternally in perfect communion with the Father, prayer was something Jesus prioritized. We are going to look at Jesus' teaching on prayer in Matthew 6:5–15. Here, among His core instructions, is Christ's "how-to" on talking with God. It really doesn't get better than this!

Matthew 5–7 is the Sermon on the Mount—in most of our Bibles these three chapters are wall-to-wall red letter. In my text, only the headings are in black; everything else is straight from Jesus. We can think of these chapters as the central collection of guidelines for authentic living, taught by the Master.

Jesus begins by acknowledging how much prayer is *not* authentic. He wants His disciples to practice prayer under certain directions we can discover with the seven questions below. Use them as you evaluate the current health of your prayer life.

Is my prayer real?

By that phrasing, I don't mean, is it real prayer? I mean, is my prayer genuine, sincere—authentic? Any of those words would work in that question.

Jesus began in Matthew 6:5, **"And when you pray,** (not *if* but *when*) **you must not be like the hypocrites. For they love to stand and pray in the synagogues and at the street corners, that they may be seen by others. Truly, I say to you, they have received their reward."** The word translated *hypocrites*, as we mentioned in the first chapter, comes from the theater. It described a person who was good at acting, mimicking, and appearing to be something they were not. Accumulated Jewish traditions in the time of Jesus had reduced prayer from meaningful, spontaneous, sincere communication with God and had made it into rote prayers at certain times, on set occasions; a form without a function; a ritual. "This is when we pray. These are the words we say. We repeat them over and over again." They were left with ritualistic, monotonous, and mind-numbing prayer.

Notice He says, **"And when you pray, you must not be like the hypocrites. For they** (don't miss this) **love to stand ..."** (v. 5). Now there are two words in Greek for *standing*. One word conveys an uncertain or timid stance. The other word for *stand* means *to take your place, mark your spot,* and *make your stand*. Now these hypocrites, they *love* to stand. Which one of those *stands* do you think Jesus uses? Correct, the second one. Hypocrites love to boldly take their place. They think, "Only two more people and it's my turn to pray. Only one more person and I'm up! Very soon I'll take the stage and everybody's going to be listening to me talk to God. They will be so impressed with me this week at small group. I'm going to blow them away with my prayer. Revival will break out! Because I am so awesome at talking to God!" The hypocrites got an emotional rush out of displaying their holiness **"They love to stand and pray in the synagogues."**

Oh, and not just in the synagogues, but **"... and on the street corners."** In today's language, "I love to get to my office early. I can hardly wait when I'm at my desk with my Bible open and people walk by and see me. I'm so godly." Or, "I love when my kids come downstairs in the morning and see Mom with her coffee and her Bible open. They're seeing how good I am at God. I've finally got the God thing figured out."

Really?! Because Jesus says if that's the part you like—the impression you create—then you have your reward.[5] Whatever that's doing for you, those feelings are the only result, because the performance is not doing anything for God. He is not responding to you. "Why doesn't God answer my prayers?" Well, it could be because you love it when people see you being spiritual. If your public prayer exceeds your private prayer, and if you prefer it that way, well, you can see how Jesus goes on here.

"Truly, I say to you, they have received their reward. But when you pray, go into your room and shut the door . . ." (v. 5). How clear is that? This is prayer by yourself. It's not wrong to pray in groups. It's good to pray as couples. It's important to pray in your small group; a man with a man, a woman with a woman. But all this needs to be the overflow of what's happening in secret. If the substance of your prayer life is your public prayers; if your high watermark is people hearing you pray, that's not great.

Here's the furnace for an authentic prayer life: **"Go into your room and shut the door . . ."** (v. 6). Stop thinking, "Well, I hope my kids grow up and say they saw Dad praying." I hope our kids grow up and say, "Dad never put on a show of praying, but I knew he prayed."

> THE SECRET TO PRAYER IS PRAYER IN SECRET.

Once you are alone with God, **"pray to your Father who is in secret. And your Father who sees in secret will reward you"** (v. 6). The prayer closet allows no showing off. Solitary prayer is a mark of your sincerity, only seen by you. Who goes by themselves into a room with the door closed and gets on their knees to fake it? No one does that! No one *pretends* in secret.

Get this: the secret to prayer is prayer in secret. And as painful as it is to say it, the litmus test for the vitality of your spiritual life is what is happening in that private place that only you and God know about. Everything else that happens in your spiritual life, if it's genuine, is rooted in what goes on just between you and God. Wow!

What God *doesn't* want is these repetitious, over and over, same-thing prayers. Followers of Jesus can't afford to let their prayer lives degenerate into some kind of mush. We actually get to talk to our Creator, the Maker of heaven and earth!

Most religions promote some kind of praying, and many teach you to choose a prayer (even the prayer in this passage) and say it over and over. Hypnotize yourself or God with mindless repetition. Make a little piece of jewelry you can use to count your cycles. "BLLLLLLIT. Did it! BLLLLLLIT. Did it! BLLLLLIT. Done!" God hates the formulaic approach to talking with Him! He wants to hear from the real you. Which gets to this next question ...

Is my prayer simple?

"And when you pray, do not heap up empty phrases as the Gentiles ..." (v. 7). It looks like our ancestors had a reputation. The pagan Gentiles in general practiced polytheism, so they had a lot of deities to juggle. For them, praying involved coping with the demands of all these gods. Each god had a weakness or fault they had to take into account. Prayers became rote incantations designed to keep the gods happy and distracted. But if the gods aren't real and the idols are powerless, then it follows that the phrases said to them are empty, no matter how high we might stack them up!

Now, back to Jesus' instructions: **"And when you pray, do not heap up empty phrases as the Gentiles do, for they think that they will be heard for their many words"** (v. 7). They think, "Well, this God is going to like it if I say it one more time. If I persist, God's going to hear me." We can see this in the story in 1 Kings 18:17–40 where the pagan priests went head to head with Elijah in a prayer contest. He was outnumbered 400 to 1. Each side was going to call down fire from heaven. Elijah said, "The prayers that bring the fire down are getting through to the real God. The other one is an impostor. This is about your god Baal and my God YHWH; may the true God win." Then Elijah added, "You go first."

So the priests **"called upon the name of Baal** (which is to say Satan, though they didn't realize it) **from morning until noon, saying 'O Baal,**

answer us!' (v. 26). It was what we call today a mantra: "O Baal, answer us," over and over. During the lunch break, Elijah **"mocked them, saying, 'Cry aloud, for he is a god. Either he is musing, or he is relieving himself, or is on a journey, or perhaps he is asleep and must be awakened'"** (v. 27). So they cried louder! They chanted 'O Baal, answer us,' hour after hour. Actually, **"they raved on until the time of the offering of oblation** (evening sacrifice)**"** (v. 29). After a full day of this circus, it was time to get real. Elijah prepared his sacrifice and doused it with water. Then he simply and calmly, one time, invited God Almighty to do His thing: **"Then the fire of the LORD fell and consumed the burnt offering and the wood and the stones and the dust, and licked up the water that was in the trench"** (v. 38).

As with Elijah, the answers to prayer don't come from some sort of obnoxious echo like a child who thinks he can wear down a parent through incessant repetition. Lose that. I wonder what all of our prayers sound like in heaven when they go on and on? Let's be clear on this. The issue *isn't* that we can only mention something to God one time. We can talk to God as often as something is on our heart and mind. But the issue *is* our thinking that incessant repetition will force God's hand.

I have three wonderful children. After two boys, having a daughter has been quite an experience for me. Somehow it's always been harder to say no to my daughter. When she comes and asks (she sent me a text this morning), "Dad, I need something," of course, I say (I texted her back), "No problem." Her request was so reasonable and I want to respond. When she comes to me for something, she's not like, "Dad? I just want to tell you I thank you for being my dad. And I'm so glad I have a dad who's a father like you. And I appreciate so much knowing you're here with me now, Dad, as I'm about to work around to ask . . ."

At that point, if I had hair, I'd be pulling it out: "What do you want!?" But isn't that sometimes the way we talk to God? God loves you and me, yet do we approach Him like we believe it?

Romans 8:14–15 says we should come to Him as Abba Father and make our requests known to Him—simply and directly. In fact, here in the Matthew 6 text, **"And when you pray, do not heap up empty phrases as the Gentiles do, for they think that they will be heard for their**

> PRAYERS DO NOT INFORM GOD. PRAYERS EXERCISE FAITH IN GOD.

many words. Do not be like them, for your Father knows what you need before you ask him" (vv. 7–8).

Make a note of this: Prayers do not inform God. Prayers exercise faith in God. God knows what you need before you ask. No one has ever uttered a prayer where God said, "Oh! *Now* I see!" We don't unburden our hearts before God so He can understand! We unburden our hearts to God so we can have the experience of *hearing* Him understand, of knowing ourselves that He knows even though He knows before we ask.

Now, don't leap to the false idea that God's foreknowledge makes our prayers needless. Don't say, "If He knows, then I don't need to tell Him." True, He doesn't *need* to learn what's on your heart, but *you* need to tell Him! You are exercising your faith in Him as you pray.

Is my prayer worshipful?

We have now arrived in familiar territory, the Lord's Prayer itself. Jesus graciously says, **"Pray then like this"** (v. 9). This short phrase is where people often make a mistake. Jesus wants us to pray, not pray *this* prayer. *Pray* is the command word, but *like* is the control and direction term. Pray *like* this. Jesus didn't mean, "Recite this prayer," or, "Pray a prayer with this many words," or even, "Pray a prayer with these kinds of phrases." Actually, I believe this prayer provides us with *categories* of praying. As in, "When you pray, keep these categories in mind." Jesus prayed for a very long time in the garden of Gethsemane. He didn't spend the evening before His crucifixion saying the Lord's Prayer over and over again. There are categories of praying and each of the lines in the Lord's Prayer points to one of the categories. The first line in the prayer relates to the question before us: Is my prayer worshipful?

"Pray then like this: 'Our Father in heaven, hallowed be your name'" (v. 9). The first words are significant: **Our Father.** According to Jesus, we can address God as Father. We *should* address God in prayer as our Father. This is corrective for me. Over time we can develop some bad prayer habits. I realized when I listened to old recorded sermons that I often began my prayers, "God, we just—" Incorrect. Don't you want the Word of God to correct you? I'm no longer going to pray like that. Jesus was fairly clear about this. We are not supposed to call any human being Father, and we are supposed to call God our Father.

Also, we pray *to* the first person of the Trinity, not to the second person of the Trinity. Jesus gives us access to God the Father through prayer in His name. We do not pray to Jesus; we follow Jesus' lead and pray to the Father. It is more biblical to picture Jesus accompanying you into God the Father's presence than to direct your prayers to Jesus.[5] If you think that prayer to Jesus is more intimate than prayer to the Father, you're wrong about your perception. Your Father in heaven is the One who meets your needs.

People say, "But James, I didn't have a very good father."

Well, then God wants to—through the Scriptures and by His Spirit—correct your understanding and give you a better experience.

You say, "Well my father only wanted to take stuff from me. He hurt me. My father . . . my father . . ." I'm sorry about your disappointment and pain. But isn't it wonderful that you have a Father in heaven who loves you, longs to hear from you, and wants to give good things to you, His child? What better antidote for the problem of failed human fathering than a Father in heaven who loves you?

Pray like this: Our Father. I've challenged our church about this practice. No more starting your prayer with "God. . ." We don't begin our prayers with, "Jesus . . ." for sure. Let's let God's Word shape our thinking as we pray.

I grew up hearing my mother and father say, "Our Father . . ." Actually, I remember my dad saying, "Father in heaven . . ." Do you want to be like Jesus? Pray like Him, to the Father.

And then notice the next phrase: **"... hallowed be your name."** The word *hallowed* is a wonderful, old English term that means *to make holy; separate; infinitely pure, righteous*. It describes God as *perfect in all He says and does*. We don't *make* God holy; He *is* holy. Our prayers express recognition. We are saying, "May You be recognized for who You are—absolutely holy." Now *that's* a category of praying.

The name of God has to do with God's person and reputation. When David acknowledged, **"He leads me in paths of righteousness for his name's sake,"**[6] he was reminding us that God's reputation is at stake when we trust Him. God has also revealed Himself to us through His names. The primary name of God in the Old Testament language is *YHWH* (usually pronounced *Yahweh*).[7] Some have wrongly voiced that as *Jehovah*, guessing the vowels, since Hebrew writing only uses consonants. But the Jews wouldn't even write it or speak God's name lest they be found to be using it in vain and breaking the third commandment.[8]

YHWH is God's primary name, meaning, I AM. But all through the Old Testament, God the Father adds hyphenated qualities to His name: YHWH-(some awesome trait). I want to review eight of those expanded names of God that can amplify your prayers so that when you pray, **"hallowed be your name,"** the expression can be filled with meaning rather than just repeating the words. These eight name expansions will give you more than a week's worth of daily reflections on the way God's name is hallowed by who He is and what He does. "Father in heaven, I want Your name to be exalted and adored in my life, in my family, and in every place."

When you open your Bible, remember the capital *L-O-R-D* stands for Yahweh in English Scripture. Each of the following names is a hyphenated addition to LORD:

1. *Tsikenu* = The LORD, our Righteousness

First, *YHWH-Tsikenu*. This Hebrew term is used many times in the Old Testament. Here's a memorable one: **"Behold, the days are coming, declares the LORD, when I will raise up for David a righteous Branch, and he shall reign as king and deal wisely, and shall execute justice and** righteousness in the land. In his days Judah will be saved, and Israel will dwell securely. And this is the name by which he will be called: 'The LORD is our righteousness.'"[9] *Yahweh-Tsikenu* . . . the LORD, our righteousness. "I AM your righteousness" is what the title means. This name is a life-changing thought. Consider how often you and I withhold ourselves from the place of prayer because we have felt unworthy. You have failed. You've fallen. You have stumbled in some way. And you feel ashamed about an attitude you've had or a choice you've made. So you hold yourself back from the place of prayer as though somehow you don't qualify to talk to God. And yet the Bible teaches through faith in Jesus Christ we have the righteousness of Christ imputed to us. Our standing—our qualification—to come before a holy God is not based on our own performance. It's a fact: when God looks at me, He looks at me *through* the righteousness of Christ. What an awesome motivation, not to pull back but to lean toward the Lord and say, "Father in heaven, hallowed be Your name, Yahweh-Tsikenu. You are my righteousness. You are the reason that I can come before You in prayer today. You saved us, **'not because of works done by us in righteousness, but according to his** [Your] **own mercy, by the washing of regeneration and renewal of the Holy Spirit.'"**[10] That's a worshipful prayer. You should be able to expand on the thought for several minutes as you consider who you are and who He is and the access you have because of your faith in Him.

2. *M'kaddesh* = The LORD, our Sanctification

YHWH-M'kaddesh means The LORD, our Sanctification. **"Keep my statutes and do them; I am the LORD who sanctifies you."**[11] In other words, "I AM (YHWH- M'kaddesh) the One who is changing you." When you feel like only supergodly people can pray confidently, but not regular folks like you, you couldn't be more wrong. The biblical message is that God is sanctifying—transforming—you. If you are a follower of Jesus Christ, God is working on you. He's changing you. You might not be what you could be, and you might not be what you should be, *but in Christ you are no longer what you were!*

But you say, "James, sometimes I just feel like I'm three steps forward and two steps back." Let's step forward. God is at work in your life. He is the One who sanctifies you. You can't sanctify yourself any more than you can save yourself. Your performance this week is not a statement about whether you should be praying or not. And if you feel like you're struggling? All the *more* reason to get before God in prayer.

3. *Shammah* = The LORD is there

YHWH Shammah: the LORD is there. The last verse in the book of Ezekiel offers great hope. God was describing through His prophet a time when His people would return from captivity. They would confess their sin and cease their backsliding. They would return to the Lord. They would rebuild the city, the walls, and the temple itself. God takes a verbal snapshot of His city and says, **"The circumference of the city shall be 18,000 cubits. And the name of the city from that time on shall be, The LORD Is There."**[12]

"Hallowed be your name." You get alone with God behind a closed door. I have faith to believe you're going to put this into practice this week. You are actually going to get with the Lord and kneel down before Him to say, "My Father in heaven, hallowed be Your name. Thank You that You are *YHWH-Shammah*; that You are here with me!" What an awesome promise! And God will be present there with you, listening, leaning down from heaven to hear what's on your heart and mind.

4. *Shalom* = The LORD, our Peace

YHWH-Shalom the LORD, our Peace. Do you have a place where you meet with God? Yes, you can talk to Him anywhere and at any time, but have you chosen a place you return to again and again, to meet with God? **"Then Gideon built an altar there to the LORD and called it, The LORD Is Peace."**[13] Maybe you have been tossing and turning back and forth, thinking, "How am I going to handle this?" And "I don't know if I can go forward?" Your heart is in turmoil. You need to get alone, on your knees, and say, "My Father in heaven, You are the LORD, my peace. You are the

One who calms the troubled waters in me. I don't need to get out of bed every morning and make it all work. You are the One who makes it all work. You are my Peace." Anywhere you meet God your Father becomes a place of peace, but I also recommend finding a place where you make it a habit to meet with God and find the peace only He can give.

5. *Raphah* = The LORD, our Healer

You are my Healer. *YHWH-Raphah*. In Exodus 15:26 (NKJV) God said, **"if you diligently heed the voice of the LORD . . . I will put none of these diseases on you that I have brought on the Egyptians. For I am the LORD who heals you."** We have a God who heals.

I've been tracking my PSA (Prostate Specific Antigen) count since my prostate cancer. After treatment, every six months it went down, down, down, down. Then I recently had a test and the count went up again. But they tell us that fluctuations in PSA numbers are a very common thing. That's even an indication the cancer cells are leaving your body. So I have all the reasons to be encouraged. But I confess I liked it a lot better when the count was going down. Now I'm facing six or twelve months of "You are the Lord who heals. You are YHWH-Raphah." And I trust the Lord completely.

There's a young woman in our church who got some very serious test results. We are praying with her, "Our Father, in heaven, hallowed be Your name, Your special name, I Am the LORD who Heals." We don't know why sometimes God allows sickness. Job lost everything and got sick. Paul struggled with an illness. And we don't believe we can demand healing from God. And yet our son Luke should have died in a car accident. His neck broke in three places. We believe the Lord healed and restored him in answer to the prayers of the people in our church. Our son Landon almost died before he came home from the hospital when he was born, but the Lord who heals intervened. Those are two personal stories. We have many, many accounts of healing in our church. I don't know what the Lord's will is for the sickness in your family or an illness you might be facing. But I'll tell you: you don't want to leave this matter of prayer unexplored.

James 4:2 says, **"You do not have, because you do not ask."** Often prayer is the source of God's bringing upon us what we desire for His glory. Sometimes we ask in prayer and God doesn't answer the way we prayed. But He always answers. And when the answer includes the hard way ahead, God gives the grace and strength we need as we trust Him. We don't know what the Lord's will is in every situation. But we do pray: Our Father in heaven, YHWH-Raphah—the Lord who Heals.

6. *Jireh* = The LORD, our Provider

We used to sing a song, *Jehovah-Jireh*, that included the meaning of the name: my Provider. That title comes to us from Genesis 22:14, **"And Abraham called the name of place The LORD will provide."** I had a personal conversation with someone who reads almost all of the Friendship Registers in our church. And she said, "I'll tell you what stands out in those weekly notes: People have needs. People are looking for work. Folks are *hurting*." And this is in our church. We have a God who provides and we should be a people who trust Him.

When the apostle Paul gave the Philippians a short outline for prayer, the highpoint of the process was the assurance that God the Provider would bring peace. Notice the progression: **"Rejoice! . . . The Lord is at hand; do not be anxious about anything, but in everything by prayer and supplication with thanksgiving let your requests be made known to God. And the peace of God, which surpasses all understanding, will guard your hearts and your minds in Christ Jesus."**[14] When we pray, we can expect God the provider to do **"far more abundantly than all that we ask or think,"**[15] and we can always count on His provision of peace.[16]

7. *Nissi* = The LORD, our Banner

YHWH-*Nissi* reminds us of the LORD, our Banner. **"And Moses built an altar and called its name The LORD Is My Banner."**[17] In ancient warfare soldiers would go into battle under banners—this would have been a good job if you were in the Hebrew/Israelite army. Most of the warriors carried weapons and went toe-to-toe with the enemy as they fought for their nation. But a few soldiers had the job of standing on the hillside and holding up a massive banner. Some of these could be seen from a mile away. So the army would be fighting and they would look up and see on the hillside that banner and would remember: The LORD Will Fight for You. The sight of that banner empowered them. They continued to fight.

When God says, "I AM your Banner," I don't know what battles you're facing in your life, but the idea that God is your Banner is an awesome comfort. So if you're in the trenches and feel surrounded but you then remember God Himself is your Banner, wouldn't that make a difference? You don't have some sign, banner, or flag hanging over you; you have the Lord Himself as Banner over your life. Whatever your uncertainties and whatever is facing you as it relates to your future, the Lord is your Banner. I can't wait to get home today and get on my knees and say, "My Father in heaven, hallowed be Your name. You are the Lord, my Banner! You are all I need; all I long for; and all I seek. You are the One who hangs over my life and assures me those things, for Your glory, can be a reality."

8. *Rohi* = The LORD, our Shepherd

YHWH-Rohi comes from Psalm 23:1. "My Father in heaven, hallowed be Your name. You are **'The LORD, my Shepherd.'** You just don't work for me; You care for me. Father, You don't just carry my burdens; You carry me. You are the Lord, my Shepherd. Hallowed be Your name."

Every one of these titles waits just beyond "Hallowed be Your name" and allows us to go deeper into this God who is All in All for us. In the categories of prayer, worship is central, and holding God's name in reverence and awe brings immeasurable worship to our real, simple prayers.

Is my prayer submissive?

In all prayer, there is submission. A men's conference recently here at Harvest reminded me of the power of submission. There is something awesome (a word I try to only use in reference to who God is and what He does) about being in a roomful of men who are submitting themselves to

God and saying, "I want what God wants for my life." God longs to see the sense of community surrender from all of us together—men and women—when we are living in obedience to His will and His way for our life.

Submission is the category of prayer we are entering when we say, **"Your kingdom come, your will be done, on earth as it is in heaven."**[18] When I hear the Lord's Prayer recited in various settings, those leading usually emphasize the words *kingdom* and *will*. So it sounds like, "Your *kingdom* come, Your *will* be done . . ." That's not it. You can subtly change the meaning of something by altering what you accentuate. We should be praying "*Your* kingdom come! *Your* will be done!" Whose kingdom, mine or God's? (God's) Whose will, mine or God's? (God's) That's one of the things going on in prayer—submitting our will and our territory to God. You bring your burden before God, not as an equal but seeking and expecting *His* will to be done and *His* kingdom to prevail. Your testimony will be, "When I started to pray about this, I was praying the way *I* saw things. But as the weeks became months, I started praying differently because I came to see things *God's* way. That reality changed what I asked for and the way I asked."

> SOMETIMES PRAYER CHANGES THINGS. AND SOMETIMES PRAYER CHANGES *ME*.

Sometimes prayer changes things. And sometimes prayer changes *me*. And I start to pray more in line with what God wants than what I want. Prayer is part of the furnace God uses to fabricate His will. Praying puts us where He can work on us. It's so important to include *Your* will be done.

I'll use a medical example again. You get some negative test results from the doctor. The news is hard to hear. The boulder that drops on your life is heavy to bear. You huddle together with friends but they can't help you be okay with that. Even your family can't help you accept hard news. Ultimately, only the Lord can help you cope with whatever looms over your life. Even Jesus Christ, as He faced the cross, prayed, **"Father, if you are willing, remove this cup away from me. Nevertheless, not my will, but yours, be done."**[19] He was saying, "If it is possible, take this cup away from Me. If it is not possible, Your will be done." And finally, **"Shall I not drink the cup that the Father has given me?"**[20] Jesus showed us that sometimes praying "*Your* kingdom come, *Your* will be done" will take everything we've got.

Prayer changes you as you submit to God. You don't just come before Him with orders, "God, we're kind of over here at A; and we need You to move it to B, ASAP." Yes, **"Casting all your anxieties on him, because he cares for you,"**[21] for sure, but in the process of unburdening your heart to God about them, God's Spirit is working on you. You gradually understand what God is showing you: "You're close. I'm going to handle your concern, but my answer is more over here. You're going to have to adjust by 31 degrees and then we'll be on the same program." Even Jesus Christ in His humanity needed an adjustment. And we need it, too.

Is my prayer submissive? In what way was your last prayer submissive?

Now, you say, "But James, there are a lot of promises in God's Word about, **'Therefore I tell you, whatever you ask in prayer, believe that you have received it, and it will be yours.'**[22] And doesn't John tell us, **'And if we know that he hears us in whatever we ask, we know that we have the requests that we have asked of him.'**[23] How does that work?" Study those passages more closely. Every promise in Scripture that seems to be unqualified is, in fact, conditional. Here are the qualifiers: Jesus said, **"If you abide in me and my words abide in you, ask whatever you wish, and it will be done for you"**[24] So everybody concludes, "Jesus said, 'Ask whatever you want and it will be done for you!'" Back up! **"If you abide in me and my words abide in you"** comes first. When you get yourself to a place of true submission to God, you can ask whatever you want to because you won't ask for dumb stuff.

Sooner or later, we all have to learn how submission comes before wide-open prayer. Let's just be honest about our praying. Many of us ask for silly and selfish things. Or maybe it isn't something dumb; maybe we just insist to God, "This is the way that I would do it." But God doesn't rule by committee. So in prayer I'm submitting and aligning my will with God. I have to bring both my faith and will to the table when I meet with God:

Faith —Believing, trusting, and letting His words abide in me—these are all ways of saying the same thing: submission. When I pray by faith, "Father in heaven," I am acknowledging His massive superiority in every respect over my life. And I am submitting myself by faith to what He thinks is best.

Will —When I pray according to His will, I am submitting myself. I am aligning myself and my will with Him and what He says. This happens as I let His words abide in (take up residence, renovate, change) me. Study those "whatever you ask" passages. You'll find God's guarantees about prayer are not nearly as unqualified as some people say.

In Jesus' name

The most important moment of submission comes at the end of every prayer when we say, "In Jesus' name." Don't ever get tired of saying those words. And don't miss what they mean. Every so often I'll hear someone get to the end of their prayer with just *Amen*. And I want to interrupt, "No. *In Jesus' name*, Amen!" Do not leave out that part. That's the most important component! You're not approaching God based on your authority or standing; you are coming through Christ and under His permission. Using His name is the point of submission. His name represents all that He is! And when you say, "In Jesus' name," you are yielding yourself, your will, and your prayers to your Father. When you use Jesus' signature at the close of your prayers, you are also hallowing His name.

"Father, if I don't have this right—if I'm asking amiss—I trust You to sort it out." James says, **"You do not have, because you do not ask. You ask and do not receive, because you ask wrongly, to spend it on your passions."**[25] The attitude of submission prays, "If I'm asking for wrong stuff, at the wrong time, for the wrong reasons, or in the wrong way, correct my prayer, Father, in Jesus' name." You're saying. "I submit my sense of what should be to Your sense of what will be, and when and how. In the name of Your Son, Jesus Christ . . ." I don't even say anymore "In Your name, Jesus." I'm not talking to Him. I'm talking to His Father. Jesus got me into the room and before the throne,[26] so I'm praying in Jesus' name.

Please don't ever tire of closing with Jesus' name. Understand that appealing to His name is the most precious part of your prayer. It's your submitting of yourself to God.

Back in Matthew 6, **"Your kingdom come, your will be done, on earth as it is in heaven"** (v. 10). How is it in heaven, by the way? For sure, it's awesome. But how do you suppose God's will works in heaven? If God says to the angels, "Build some more mansions." Do you think they respond, "We're tied up right now" or "We've got some supply problems and the permits aren't coming through"? I'm going to suggest that in heaven things probably happen pretty much *exactly* the way God wants, on time, every time. So when you pray, "Your will be done," you're declaring, "God, I long for it to be like it is in heaven. I want my life to reflect the state where what You want happens on time, every time." That's a prayer of submission.

Is my prayer practical?

This is so straightforward: **"Give us this day our daily bread"** (v. 11). Now that's more than a prayer for food. Our daily bread represents all the basics we require. So when you pray, "Give us this day our daily bread," your prayer is practical. Here are four essential needs covered by bread we can pray for:

Income. We can pray for adequate income for every household—not so our *wants* will be met but so our *needs* will be met. When we're praying about financial needs, we know we're praying according to God's will. Jesus tells us right in this chapter, Matthew 6:25–34, that all of our basic needs will be met. Don't worry or be concerned about **"'What shall we eat?' or 'What shall we drink?' or 'What shall we wear?'"** (v. 31). So we *know* that already. I don't have to pray, "Lord, meet my basic needs if it's Your will." Now, it might not be God's will for you to have the exact job that you're thinking about, but it *is* God's will for you to have a job. It *is* God's will for the needs in your house to be met. And you can pray boldly with those needs in mind.

We anticipate great miracle stories that come out of our church-wide weeks of prayer. God moves when His people gather to pray. People get work, problems get resolved, and awesome things happen. We are asking God to do it. And He waits to do it then so we will all know it was because we prayed and the results were connected to Him.

Physical health. God doesn't promise health to everyone. But He has promised He is the God who heals. He has never stopped being all that He is. So healing is for today. So you can pray confidently for physical health. If God has a different plan, He can reveal it to you. And no matter what the outcome, He will be with you.

Emotional health. We all have basic emotional needs. There is so much lack of wellness around us today. People are depressed and filled with anxiety, bitterness, fear, and apathy. "Father, I need my daily bread of emotional sustenance. I long to be able to handle things. I need to know I'm not going to lose it. Please give me the peace of knowing I'm going to be okay. I need You to calm the waters in my life, God, and make me a stable person. In Jesus' name." You can pray for emotional health with confidence.

Spiritual health. We can pray for the salvation of loved ones. We know God **"is not wishing that any should perish but that all should come to repentance."**[27] We can call out to God to bring wandering children back home, back to Him. We can ask Him to save our spouse and to rescue our daughter-in-law. We can call out to God for these things with assurance. These matters are all part of daily bread. There is so much ground we can cover in the category of bringing our needs before God.

Is my prayer repentant?

Authentic prayer includes repentance. **"And forgive us our debts as we also have forgiven our debtors."**[28] Now that's not a credit card prayer. It's talking about sins between people and between people and God. If I were to strike you, my blow would create a debt. I owe you now. And what we're praying here is, "Father, we have offended You, God. We have slapped You, as it were. We have created an offense. And we are asking You, God, to forgive us the same way we forgive other people who create offense with us." Really?! Is that what you mean? Is 'forgive like I forgive' the standard you want? Words like those are a hard prayer to pray: "Forgive me the way I forgive my sister, God. Do it just like that." "Take my high watermark in forgiveness and apply the same measure to me, God." Talk about your prayer changing you!? "I want to be forgiven the way I forgive other people." Because in prayer I expand my sense of how I have offended God. And I thereby lower my sense of how much others have offended me. Prayer is changing me.

Don't come to church with an attitude toward somebody and your back turned on them. "We may have gotten here in the same car, but we are not on the same program." Guarding a hard heart while we sing, "Lord, I lift Your name on high . . ." Really?! "If you come to worship," Jesus said, **"and there remember that your brother has something against you, leave your gift there before the altar and go. First be reconciled with your brother, and then come and offer your gift."**[29] When was the last time you left a worship service to seek out a brother, sister, friend to reconcile because you knew an offense was between you and them that was blocking your access to God? Repentance must be one of the categories we include in prayer.

Is my prayer expectant?

Some translations have the phrase, **"Yours is the kingdom and the power and the glory forever"**[30] and some do not. The expression is certainly biblically accurate and is now traditionally part of the Lord's Prayer.

So not only is it not wrong to close the prayer with these phrases; it's not wrong to say the Lord's Prayer in its entirety. The phrases are wonderful to pray alone or together. It's just wrong to repeat it over and over like a formula and not see how much more is there.

The essence of the Lord's Prayer is an attitude of expectation that God does hear, He draws near, and He does answer. Practicing godly anticipation is one of the disciplines of a sincere faith. Recognizing and using the categories Jesus included in His model prayer puts us on the right path for an authentic prayer life.

THE REAL THING:

Learning Hunger

AT THE TIME WE PLANTED Harvest Bible Chapel, one of the spiritual disciplines I had never yet practiced was fasting. I was vaguely aware that many followers of Jesus had used this exercise as part of their lives, but it was foreign to me. But as the weight of ministry settled on my shoulders, it became increasingly clear I would need to pursue every avenue of communion with God. I began to experiment not only with prayer but also with fasting. The two became intertwined for me. I was being stretched into a deeper understanding of prayer, and fasting was an almost unavoidable part of spiritual growth. One of the biblical provocations to explore this discipline came from Jesus' comment, **"However, this kind does not go out except by prayer and fasting."**[1] Jesus was saying there are some hills to climb or obstacles to overcome that will require fasting.

I remember a weeklong fast in the early days of Harvest. I was using a rented office space a little larger than a refrigerator box, and we were meeting for worship in a high school facility. When our church plant was surviving week to week, I couldn't imagine we would eventually own over a million square feet of ministry space and all the rest God has done over the last two decades. God knew it; I was clueless. I was simply longing to be faithful with the challenges immediately before me. That awareness was plenty to make me recognize how badly I needed God's help.

Desperation had driven me to a seven-day, water-only fast. On day five or six I remember walking up a winding stairway to the second floor of the rickety, old building that housed our offices and falling on the stairs in weakness. Part of it was physical, but a major part of it was the spiritual realization of how little I had to offer. I found myself crying out to God for this church that was a dream and a call. I prayed where I was, asking God to work in me and through me to accomplish what He wanted. I couldn't say what I was offering Him, but I was all His. And I distinctly recall the sense that came over me of the Spirit communing with my spirit, "It's enough, James."

The lesson was a significant resolution of what I had discovered was my main struggle in fasting. When I proscribed a certain length to a fast, I had found at a certain point (whether it was a daylong fast or a weeklong one), my attention was being diverted to the winding down of the clock until the fast was over rather than staying focused on the reason I was fasting. Now, I fast with the expectation that God can tell me when I've gone long enough. Either the situation over which I am fasting is resolved or the Spirit releases me. I've found great benefit in considering this spiritual discipline a regular part of my walk with God.

CHAPTER FOUR

THE DISCIPLINE OF FASTING

The spiritual discipline we will look at in this chapter is one most people—even many people who have a sincere faith—do not practice. This is the discipline of fasting. I asked one of the men I respect most in Christ today, "Have you ever fasted?" His faith has been a great example to me. I'm sure you'd recognize his name.

He said, "No. I never have."

I was stunned. "Never?!"

He said, "Never!" in a way that made it clear he wasn't considering fasting any time in the near future. Given his amazing ministry, I could only wonder what the results might have been if tempered by fasting. But he's not the first I've met. You may be one of those Christians for whom fasting sounds a lot like dieting and not so much about spiritual discipline, but I trust what follows will be a wake-up call for you.

In fact, this will help with the importance of fasting. We surveyed 100 people and have listed the top five answers to this question: Name the average Christian's most frustrating spiritual problem. What discourages and exasperates Christians more than anything else?

1   XXXXXXXXXXXXXXXXX
2   XXXXXXXXXXXXXXXXX
3   XXXXXXXXXXXXXXXXX
4   XXXXXXXXXXXXXXXXX
5.   **INCONSISTENT QUIET TIME**

Too many Christians admit, "I know I should walk with God. I want to read the Bible. I know I should pray. I want to do it. Sometimes I use a study guide. Once in a while I get into a rhythm and make myself do it. But the fact of the matter is, seven days go by and my score is zero. Sometimes it's one or two. Always hit or miss. I've been consistently inconsistent in spending time with God! And it hasn't been an occasional struggle for weeks or months; it's been my pattern for years—even decades. I know the right. I *want* the right. But I don't *choose* the right."

The average Christian's fourth most frustrating spiritual problem:

1   XXXXXXXXXXXXXXXXX
2   XXXXXXXXXXXXXXXXX
3   XXXXXXXXXXXXXXXXX
4   **I DON'T SENSE GOD'S PRESENCE WITH ME**
5.   INCONSISTENT QUIET TIME.

"I don't sense God's presence with me. I sense it at church. I feel it occasionally in other places, but mostly my life is really secular. I don't think about God all the time. I don't see God at work. I don't notice God in my home much. I wonder, 'are we really very different than our neighbors?' Why don't we sense God's presence more when we love Him as we do?"

A lack of sensing God's presence is frustrating to many people.

The average Christian's third most frustrating spiritual problem.

1   XXXXXXXXXXXXXXXXX
2   XXXXXXXXXXXXXXXXX

3   **I FEEL LIKE I DON'T MEASURE UP**

4   I DON'T SENSE GOD'S PRESENCE WITH ME.

5.   INCONSISTENT QUIET TIME.

"I have nagging areas of secret sin, attitudes I can't shake. I have anger inside. I hold bitterness and it eats away at me. I struggle with fear and anxiety. I have sinful habits constantly tripping me up. In lots of ways, God has grown me, but in certain parts of life I wonder if I've progressed at all."

The average Christian's second most frustrating spiritual problem:

1   XXXXXXXXXXXXXXXXXX

2   **NOT SEEING THE ANSWERS TO PRAYER/MIRACLES**

3   I FEEL LIKE I DON'T MEASURE UP.

4   I DON'T SENSE GOD'S PRESENCE WITH ME.

5.   INCONSISTENT QUIET TIME.

Maybe you've found yourself voicing this prayer: "Where are the miracles, Lord? Where is the answered prayer? I mean, the Bible is filled with amazing stories. I would just like . . . how about one for me, God? I hear other Christians have breakthroughs, specific needs they've prayed about. But I feel like I've asked You for a lot of things in the last few months. And I'm just not seeing that much of You in action." The disappointment many followers of Jesus feel about the effectiveness of their prayers leads directly to the number one issue:

The average Christian's most frustrating spiritual problem.

1   **PRAYER TIME**

2   NOT SEEING THE ANSWERS TO PRAYER/MIRACLES

3   I FEEL LIKE I DON'T MEASURE UP.

4   I DON'T SENSE GOD'S PRESENCE WITH ME.

5.   INCONSISTENT QUIET TIME.

Does this sound familiar? "My prayer time—what's that? As I was reading the last chapter on prayer, I determined I was going to do better. And

I set out to spend an hour in prayer. I didn't do it. I sat here and thought, 'I'm going to find a prayer meeting where I can join others in calling out to God.' But I didn't do that either. I wanted to. I agreed it was right. But I've got to be honest, James. I read the last chapter and my prayer life since hasn't been in any way different than it was the week before I read it. It's frustrating because I look into my heart and I can almost hear the verdict: 'You don't change because you don't want to.'"

Now your conclusion is not correct! The problem is—in this regard— *not* that you don't *want* to engage with God in conversation; the problem is, even though in your heart you feel like you want to, you want other things *more.*

What are we to do when the things we want deepest down don't end up becoming our reality, but the quick things—the easy things, the accessible things—those are the things we end up choosing. The problem is, somehow we are just not getting from *knowing* what's best to *doing* what's best. We feel stuck.

Now God has given us some tools to break these patterns. But even these strategies require *wanting to*, a desire willing to act. Study of God's Word would help me break these habits; Scripture memory and time in God's Word; time in prayer—other disciplines we're going to get to in the chapters to come. But what has God given you and me to break the pattern of *not doing the things that we most and deeply want to do?*

Answer: fasting.

I would challenge you to flip to the little section at the back of your Bible that lists words. Look up the terms *fast, fasted, fasting.* Consult a Bible concordance if you want; they are all over the place for free on the Internet. You will be *shocked* at how frequently the subject of fasting comes up in Scripture. It's throughout both Testaments. Jesus fasted regularly. He even fasted for forty days and forty nights before He launched His three-year ministry.

Let's get a definition in front of us before we dig into this spiritual discipline. Fasting: *Abstaining from food for measured periods of time in order to heighten my hunger for the things of God.* Read that definition again.

You respond, "But James, I'm *not* that hungry for God. What's the solution for that?" In developing the disciplines of a sincere faith, the solution to stirring a hunger for God is fasting. Matthew 5:6 says, **"Blessed are those who hunger and thirst for righteousness, for they shall be satisfied."** Jesus exposed a core problem we have. Let's identify that problem and then work toward a solution.

WE HAVE LITTLE HUNGER FOR GOD

True that! "But wait," you say, "James, I don't know if it's really true. I *am* reading this book! Isn't that showing some hunger?"

I'm saying we have little hunger for God in comparison to what we could and should have. And even if you have more hunger for God than most, how is your consistency of hunger going? Not many people missed a meal this week. But how frequently do we miss spiritual meals?

By little hunger for God, I mean little in amount, in consistency, and, most of all, in proportion. I have yet to meet anyone who could stand up and say, "Actually, I do have a hunger for God that *is* proportionate to how awesome He is and what He offers. My desire for God is right in line with how great He is." Even the most passionate followers reading these pages would have to acknowledge, "How awesome God is *dwarfs* my hunger for Him. It's really hard to explain how He always far exceeds my longing to know Him." So look again at Matthew 5:6, where Jesus said, **"Blessed are those who hunger and thirst for righteousness, for they shall be satisfied."** The word *blessed* shows up nine times in the first eleven verses of Matthew 5. It means *happy, contented, satisfied,* and *fulfilled.* There aren't many of these happy, satisfied, blessed people in our world. And far too few in the church of Christ, in our church at Harvest, are really blessed in the way that Jesus talked about here. But why?

"Blessed are they who hunger and thirst for righteousness . . ." Let me ask you a personal question. When was the last time you were hungry? I'm talking about a physical desire for food. Now? Good answer. I'm going to make that worse before we're done.

When you *are* hungry, how long are you hungry? For me, sometimes twenty minutes, if I'm stuck in a meeting or traffic. But I keep a snack bar in my briefcase just in case I —

Now honestly, how much do we really know of hunger? I mean, we feel a little twinge and we run for the kitchen. The vast majority of us who live in the West—I'm just speaking in general terms—don't have any real extended experience with deprivation. Even if you are hungry in a long meeting, you're going to get it settled in about hour and a half maximum, probably less if you need to. Food is everywhere. It's accessible in confusing and even unhealthy quantities. We have little firsthand awareness and understanding of even the concept of hunger.

But I can almost hear my reader say, "Prove it to me."

Food has changed significantly in the last few decades—certainly in my lifetime and in my children's lifetime. Here are just some basic statistics.

In 1990, two slices of pepperoni pizza contained 550 calories. Today, two slices of the average pepperoni pizza, size and what's put in it, weigh in at 850 calories. That's a difference of 300 calories.

"Oh, three hundred calories? What does that matter?"

Well actually, if you just consumed those 300 calories twice a month and didn't change anything else in your diet, today's pizza would put on two extra pounds a year or forty pounds over the next twenty years—which is my testimony, in essence. Funny for you!

In 1990, the average movie theater popcorn bucket provided 270 calories. If you go to a movie today or tomorrow (and I hope you'll go to a good one if you do), the same counter, the same order, "I'll take a large popcorn." It now has 630 calories.

This will get you: In 1990, the average fast-food burger contained 333 calories—today it has 590. Now I could push this to the point that I would injure some people, and I don't want to do that, but I'll name one of the offenders on the calorie frontier. The worst single burger readily available is the Chili's Smokehouse Bacon Triple Cheese Big Mouth Burger with jalapeño sauce—1901 calories. Our average physical weight and related problems reveal that we have a growing hunger for what does not ultimately satisfy (and might kill us). But we have little hunger for God.

Wilbur Reese, who wrote a book back in 1971 called *$3.00 Worth of God*, said this:

> I would like to buy $3 worth of God, please. Not enough to explode my soul or disturb my sleep, but just enough to equal a cup of warm milk or a snooze in the sunshine. I want ecstasy, not transformation. I want the warmth of the womb, not a new birth. I want a pound of the eternal in a paper sack, please. I would like to buy $3 worth of God.[2]

We seriously lack desire for God. And our hungers reveal this problem. John 4 gives us a very illuminating episode from the life of Christ. If you were just reading through the Bible regularly, it might not even be obvious to you how much the Bible has to say about food and fasting. But when you gather the Scripture together, there really is quite an amount of biblical information on this subject. As John puts it:

Now when Jesus learned that the Pharisees had heard that Jesus was making and baptizing more disciples than John (although Jesus himself did not baptize, but only his disciples), he left Judea and departed again for Galilee. [So that's a walk.] **And he had to pass through Samaria.** [Samaritans were half-Jews.] **So he came to a town of Samaria called Sychar, near the field that Jacob had given to his son Joseph. Jacob's well was there; so Jesus, wearied as he was from his journey, was sitting beside the well. It was about the sixth hour.** (vv. 1–6)

So they're all tired, ready for some resting. But where are the disciples? Hot road traveled: dusty feet, parched mouth, and sweaty clothes. What would you have been thinking if you had walked all that way? "I need some water and food." And so check what happens next.

"A woman from Samaria came to draw water. Jesus said to her, 'Give me a drink.' (For his disciples had gone into the town to buy food)" (v. 7). So here's this needy lady coming. But the disciples were saying, "Man! Where's the nearest Wendy's? I'm hungry enough to eat a camel!"

"I've got to talk to this lady," Jesus might have said.

"We'll talk to her when we get back. Do You know how long it's been since we've eaten? You're not coming? Well, we'll bring You take-out."

Jesus waits to minister to the woman. The disciples go running off in search of food! Their hunger was their immediate priority.

Now we'll just skip over the account of Jesus' amazing conversation with this woman. We'll visit with her again later in the book. She came to the well with a jug for water and Jesus sent her home with living water. We have two stories going on here: one about Jesus and the woman; the other about the disciples and their eating habits.

Now just a little background here. The disciples were preoccupied with food. I relate to that and to them. In Matthew 12:1, they were walking through a grain field and they got into a whole argument with the Pharisees when the disciples started breaking grain off of the stalks because they were hungry. "You can't snack on the Sabbath!"

"But we're hungry!"

So they definitely had a food thing. In Matthew 14:15, **the disciples came to him and said, '. . . send the crowds away to go into the villages and buy food for themselves,'** which was another way of saying, "*We're* hungry. *They're* hungry—but let's make sure we take care of us." In Mark 7:2, the Pharisees saw the disciples eating with unclean hands. They couldn't even wait and do the ceremonial appropriate thing. They just had to dig into the food.

And it's not like they weren't warned along the way. In Luke 12:23, Jesus rebuked them and said, **"Life is more than food."** In John 6:27, He said to them, **"Do not work for the food which perishes [spoils], but for the food which endures to eternal life."**[3] This subject of food came up a lot.

Meanwhile, back by the well outside Sychar, John 4 continues. Jesus has sent the woman away. She goes to get her husband who isn't her husband. But she meets a lot of people on the way, and she can't help but spread the news: **"'Come, see a man who told me all that I ever did. Can this be the Christ?' They went out of the town and were coming to him"** (v. 29). God has a way of redeeming the most obviously broken people and then using them to pull off authentic and effective evangelism!

Now the disciples are back from Wendy's. When they arrived, Jesus was finishing His conversation with the woman. **"They marveled that he was talking with a woman, but no one said, 'What do you seek?' or, 'Why are you talking with her?'"** (v. 27). Even though they noticed they were immediately distracted. Why? Food. **"Meanwhile the disciples were urging him saying . . ."** What are they saying to Jesus? **"Rabbi, eat!"** (v. 31).

Jesus' answer is a sermon by itself. **"But he said to them, 'I have food to eat that you do not know about'"** (v. 32). What a phenomenal statement! Yet, as we will see, the disciples missed it.

We have little hunger for God. And Jesus shows us how other hungers can further detract from our hunger for God.

WE ONLY HAVE SO MUCH HUNGER

Jesus told His disciples as they urged Him to eat, "I'm eating. I'm just focused on different nourishment than you guys. Don't be worried about Me. I'm feeding on something better than food."

Now to me, this is a very helpful concept. Please picture with me a pie (since it's your imagination at work, I'll let you choose what kind of pie it is). As you are thinking about that pie, let's let it represent your total capacity to feed. The pie is 100 percent of all your appetites.

Every day you awake and you have a certain capacity to satisfy yourself. And it's finite. It may be large, but it's not infinite. It's limited. You have a set of restricted appetites to feed and a limited amount of time and energy in which to do it.

So you get up in the morning and prepare yourself for the day. You spend a certain amount of energy on dressing. Then you have some breakfast, whatever you have for fuel in the morning. Some of us wake up, thinking, "I've got to start eating. Get it going. Coffee! Fast! I've got to have that jolt. And then I've got to feed some other need. I'll listen to the radio or iPod to entertain myself with music. Or, I just have to hear the latest on the sports network." Some people listen to news or talk. They have an audio-hunger for certain programs. "Man! That radio preacher or that commentator just fires me up!" Whatever it is. And you start to listen to something that feeds you, which might be very good, but it consumes some of your hunger reserves.

But then you have to get to work. You put a lot of energy into your job, spend a lot of your capacity—whether you are working in the home or somewhere in the marketplace. Work takes a big piece of the pie.

And then you talk on the phone. Sometimes I want to throw my phone across the universe. That wireless device is really starting to be a problem. My wife has had to get my attention so many times in the last few months: "Honey! Put that thing down!" Phones interrupt at so many levels. And now Smartphones! Who came up with that name? They have at least eight different ways to take over your life. A lot of energy goes into phone management. People with Smartphones are clearly not *that* smart (and yes, I'm one of them). I know I feel somewhat ashamed for letting my email, my texting, my tweeting, and my web search eat up a lot of my everyday pie. You and I are spending our limited capacity on these things.

And then before too long, a morning snack . . . and then lunch. Whatever you have for midday meal, you indulge. You can tell it's true because you're tired in your responsibilities in the afternoon because lunch was too large.

After your groggy afternoon, you eat dinner. More food. Then you begin the evening with some family time, I hope, if this is something you're including as an important piece of the pie. But then the TV goes on and consumes more life. You think it replenishes you, but it's one of the most draining passive activities we do. We give our time and our emotion to entertainment. The pie is almost gone. We're exhausted and spent in almost every way.

And then, just before we get into bed, we kneel down and we pray, "God, why don't I have any hunger for You?" We only have so much hunger, and if we've used up all our time and appetite for other things . . . look at how the disciples respond to Jesus.

"But he said to them, 'I have food to eat that you do not know about.' So the disciples said to one another . . ." They just didn't get it. **"Has anyone brought him something to eat?"** (vv. 32–33). They could not conceive He had not gratified His hunger for food. They thought, "Man! When we're hungry? We eat! How can He not be hungry?"

When He told them, "I'm eating a different kind of food," their immediate thought was, "Did He do a miracle?! Did He find some food? Has He been holding out on us?" Jesus heard them asking each other, **"Has anyone brought him something to eat?"** and He said to them, **"My food is to do the will of him who sent me and to accomplish his work"** (v. 34).

I can say in my life, by far, the most satisfying things that have ever happened to me have been those moments where I have sensed I have done as the Lord wanted me to do and served as He wanted me to serve; shared as He wanted me to share, and given as He wanted me to give. Those moments remind me that the attempt to satisfy self apart from doing the will of God is inevitably not only a frustrating and empty pursuit but also creates a very discouraging result.

Again, John 4:34 says, **"My food is to do the will of him who sent me and to accomplish his work."** And what *is* God's will and work, Jesus? He says it in verse 35. This is the theme verse that launched our church. **"Do you not say, 'There are yet four months, then comes the harvest'? Look, I tell you . . ."**

I remember when we started Harvest Bible Chapel. People wrote me letters—no email then—and said, "We don't need another church in the northwest suburbs of Chicago." Incorrect! We need many, many more churches still!

I'm so proud of my good friend Erwin Lutzer, who pastors the great Moody Memorial Church in downtown Chicago. Here's a godly man. I said to him before this was ever known to anyone, "Hey, Erwin. We've been given a building right downtown. It's not that far from your church. And at some point in the future—we don't know when—we're probably going to have a Harvest campus in your neighborhood."

And his answer was just like this: Three, two, one . . . "Well, that's great news, isn't it? Because there are a lot of people around here who need Christ."

Is that amazing? I mean, what a godly response. There's a man who is *feeding* on doing the will of God. Not building his reputation. Not boosting his own ego but just longing to see the gospel go out and penetrate people's lives. He's living on what Jesus was living on. He's got his eyes on the harvest, just as Jesus said: **"Do you not say, 'There are yet four months, then comes the harvest'? Look, I tell you, lift up your eyes, and see that the fields are white** (or ripe) **for harvest"** (v. 35).

We have little hunger for God.

We have only so much hunger.

So, here's the third problem:

OUR ENSLAVEMENT TO FOOD HINDERS
OUR HUNGER FOR GOD

We will return to John 4 in a minute. But first I want to draw your attention to a passage of Scripture in the Old Testament. Deuteronomy 32:15 begins, **"But Jeshurun . . ."** The name *Jeshurun* means *people of the Law*. Moses was using it as a nickname for the nation of Israel. He was describing God's people. **"But Jeshurun (God's people) grew fat and kicked; you grew fat, stout, and sleek; then he forsook God who made him and scoffed at the Rock of his salvation."**

There is a broader sense in which satisfying ourselves physically represents our efforts to take care of all appetites. Food is the subject on the table here because fasting is what we are talking about. But we understand there are many, many ways to satisfy ourselves. This isn't an attack on people who struggle in the eating category. That may not be a big deal for you through behavior or metabolism. You still need to face the same challenge: if you are satisfying yourself with that which is not bread or meat but *with other things that don't really fill your soul*, your hunger for God will be hindered.

For many of us, our enslavement to food diminishes our hunger for God. Paul, describing certain people, says their **"end is destruction, whose god is their belly . . ."**[4] It's right in the Bible. For some people (I'll go first in an effort to maintain honesty), for me sometimes, my appetite for food can quench and has quenched—I want to get out of the theoretical into the actual—my hunger for God.

I'm five weeks now into a Get Healthy physical emphasis for this year, accounting to others in the process. Not superenthused about how much progress I've made so far.

> IT'S NOT A *HOW-TO* I'M SEEKING; IT'S A *WANT TO* I FIND LACKING!

Some, but not as much as I had hoped to or want to make. Friends have offered precious encouragement. I could fill a small room with the diet plans I've received—regular stuff, nutritional stuff, all across the spectrum of weight control strategies. I love everyone who has tried to help. I'm just going to say . . . but here's the deal, yo! I don't need help with *how-to*. The how-to options are many. It's not a *how-to* I'm seeking; it's a *want to* I find lacking!

In order to get to a healthier place in this regard, there has to be a humble recognition that food (or something else, possibly, for you) is filling a place in my heart. It is supplying a strength, offering a comfort, or promising a relief that God wants to give. God won't provide as long as I'm busy trying to provide for myself elsewhere.

Now what to do about the problem when we recognize our enslavement to food (or some other appetite) hinders our hunger for God? In a sermon preached in 1562 in The Church of England, the minister said this:

The first end of fasting is to chastise the flesh so that it be not too selfish, but tamed and brought into subjection to the Spirit.

He succinctly described the purpose of fasting. And by the way, the person who carries the additional shame of being overweight is—I must say—not necessarily in a worse place. Let me just put it this way. Who's struggling with food more: the person who's stuffing donuts or the guy who is carefully weighing his sliced turkey? *Both!* is the answer. They're at opposite extremes of the same struggle!

You can be so preoccupied with your health. "I am *on* this! I have control! I am ruling over this part of me." But God is no more a part of your life than He is a part of the person who is comforting themselves with more food than they can righteously consume. Both have a problem! I note this lest we find ourselves in judgment of others instead of seeing our own place of struggle.

I love this account about Rees Howells, another UK pastor from the last century. As his biographer Norman Grubb described it,

God began to deal with a simple appetite in Rees Howells—the love of food. It was at a time when he had a great burden for a certain convention, which was being disrupted by assaults of the enemy. The Lord called him to a day of prayer and fasting, which was something new to him. Used, as he was, to a comfortable home and four good meals a day, it came as a shock to realize that it meant no dinner, and he was agitating about it. And would it only happen once? Supposing God asked him to do it every day!

When midday came he was on his knees in his bedroom, but there was no prayer that next hour. "I didn't know such a lust was in me," he said afterwards. "My agitation was the proof of the grip it had on me. If the thing had no power over me, why did I argue about it?"

At one o'clock his mother called him, and he told her he wasn't taking lunch. But she called again, as a mother would, and urged, "It won't take you long to have it." The goodly aroma from downstairs was too much for him, and down he came. But after the meal, when he returned to his room, he couldn't get back into the presence of God. He came face to face with disobedience to the Holy Ghost. "I felt I was like the man in the garden of Eden," he said. "I went up the mountain and walked miles, cursing that 'old man' within me . . ."

He didn't take dinner for many days after that, but spent the hour with God.[5]

FASTING BREAKS OUR ENSLAVEMENT TO FOOD

First Corinthians 6 gives us some more instruction on this important matter. Paul says, **"All things are lawful for me, but not all things are helpful. All things are lawful for me, but I will not be dominated by anything"** (v. 12). Anything *I must* have is enslavement for me. If I have to have a substance—legal or illegal? I'm enslaved. Do I crave my coffee in the morning? For me it would be, must I have my sugar after supper? Paul declared, **"I will not be dominated by anything."** But he wasn't finished: **"'Food is meant for the stomach and the stomach for food,' –and God will destroy both one and the other. The body is not meant for sexual immorality, but for the Lord, and the Lord for the body"** (v. 13). Sexual appetite is another area of struggle for many people. **"And God raised the Lord and will also raise us up by his power"** (v. 14). Paul is pointing not only to the problems but also to the power of God available to us in dealing with our enslavement to food and other forms of bondage.

First Corinthians 6:19–20 sharpens the issue. **"Do you not know that your body is a temple of the Holy Spirit within you, whom you have from God? You are not your own; for you were bought with a price. So glorify God in your body."** The very appetites we connect with shame, when they are under the control of God's Spirit, become ways *in* which and *for* which we give glory to God.

And then these powerful words from Peter: **"Beloved, I urge you as**

sojourners . . ."[6] What *sojourners* means is, "This is not our home." We are just visitors here. The trappings of this world are not what I'm fired up about. I don't *have* to have it all here because I'm just a sojourner, passing through.

"I urge you, as sojourners and exiles, to abstain from the passions (that could be translated *desires* or *lusts—epithumia*) **of the flesh . . ."** "Why, Peter? Why should I abstain from the desires of my flesh? There are lots of things my flesh wants that are not wrong."

His answer? They **"wage war against your soul."** The idea of *abstain* there is not forever; not even continually but for a time. This is a significant principle. Anything that would overpower you can be set aside for a time to break its enslavement. Fasting involves *setting aside* in order to clarify importance.

John Piper said, "The absence of our fasting is the measure of our contentment with the absence of Christ."[7] When we fast, that enslavement is broken and we are freed to focus our hunger upon what we really want. Not to be repetitive, but could you just read the last two sentences again? Fasting reveals the things that control us. Fasting is a reality check. It humbles us and shows us our true selves.

Richard Foster, a longtime student of the spiritual disciplines and author of *Celebration of Discipline*, said this: "Our human cravings and desires are like rivers that tend to overflow their banks; fasting helps keep them in their proper channels."[8] If control is never gained, our enslavement to food can devastate our health, our lives, and our testimonies.

A favorite story of mine is from a book of historical fiction by a man named Thomas Costain entitled *The Three Edwards*. In it he described the life of Raynald III, a fourteenth-century duke in what is now Belgium. It has taken on fresh significance for me in the context of fasting.

By the time he had assumed his title, Raynald was so obese that he was given the unflattering Latin nickname *Crassus,* a term that can mean *plump, fat*, or *gross*. We don't know what kind of a duke Raynald was, but his appetites were a problem. After a falling-out, his younger sibling

Edward orchestrated a revolt against Raynald and removed him from his role as duke.

Although Edward could have killed Raynald, he came up with a devious plan that allowed him to reign in his brother's place. He constructed a special suite for Raynald in the castle and promised him he could regain his title and property as soon as he was able to leave the room.

This would have been easy for most people, since the room had several windows and a door of near-normal size that was neither locked nor barred. The problem was Raynald's size. To regain his freedom, he needed to lose weight. But Edward knew his older brother, so each day he provided a tempting variety of delicious foods. Instead of dieting his way out of confinement and back into power, Raynald grew larger still. When Duke Edward was accused of cruelty, he had a ready answer: "My brother is not a prisoner. He may leave anytime he wishes." Raynald stayed in that room for nearly ten years and wasn't released until after Edward's death in battle. By then his health was so ruined, he died within a year himself, a prisoner of his own appetite.

Any one of our hungers has the potential of turning us into a Raynald. A doorway of freedom is before us. Fasting breaks our enslavement to food and appetites of many kinds. And here is, I believe, wonderful news to add:

FASTING CAN IGNITE OUR HUNGER FOR GOD

The key word is *can*. Fasting *can* ignite our hunger for God. It won't necessarily. You can fast for wrong reasons, in wrong ways. The prophet Zechariah said, **"Say to all the people of the land and the priests, 'When you fasted and mourned in the fifth month and in the seventh [months] for these seventy years, was it for me that you fasted?'"**[9] The easiest thing to do would be to close this book today and say, "I'm going to fast. That's how I'm going to get my weight under control. Fasting is how I'm going to stop wasting as much on food as I do." You could forego eating for a lot of reasons and *not* do it for God and not get the benefits. And don't turn fasting into a legalistic stick you use to beat up other people or measure your own spiritual superiority. Accountability should be with a few people you can trust not to be overly impressed with your progress but keep encouraging you in your failures. Paul saw all kinds of distortions among believers as he urged them to **"seek the things that are above, where Christ is, seated at the right hand of God."**[10] Colossians 2 makes it very clear the apostle was familiar with the rallying cries of pseudospirituality: **"Do not handle, Do not taste, Do not touch (referring to things that all perish as they are used)—according to the human precepts and teachings? These have indeed an appearance of wisdom in promoting self-made religion and asceticism and severity to the body, but they are of no value in stopping the indulgence of the flesh"** (vv. 21–23).

Fasting can certainly be misplaced and misused. And maybe those are reasons it hasn't had a healthy emphasis among believers. But as is often the case, we have—in not wanting to be either legalistic or hyperreligious—really forsaken the biblical teaching on this subject.

Psalm 69:10 says, **"When I wept and humbled my soul with fasting, it became my reproach."** That's not bad news; it's good news. I saw myself as I really was and began to change.

"How did you change?"

"Well, I humbled my soul with fasting. I broke the pattern I wanted to shatter through fasting. And I discovered other patterns that needed to be broken!"

Now just some basic information at the close of this chapter on the kinds of fasts we can undertake:

Normal fast. To abstain from food for spiritual purposes. While normal fasts often include avoiding various beverages (like coffee, tea, carbonated drinks) that can become habitual, fasting does not usually mean abstaining from water. You can live without food for weeks; going without water will kill you in a matter of days. There are not many details about *how* to fast throughout Scripture because it was common knowledge to the people in Bible times. And throughout much of church history, believers practiced normal fasting and introduced it to the next generation. People like John Wesley had a regular fast day each week. When Jesus was led into the wilderness for forty days, the fact that He was fasting wasn't unusual; the length of the fast was. They knew how to fast; we've forgotten the basics. The books I mentioned earlier in this chapter (John Piper's *Hunger for God* and Richard Foster's *Celebration of Discipline*) have practical guidance if you are undertaking fasting for the first time.

Partial fast. To abstain from selected items that represent areas of struggle or danger. In Daniel 10:3, Daniel said, **"I ate no delicacies, no meat or wine entered my body"** as part of a fast. Years earlier in his youth, he and his friends had adopted a largely vegetarian diet even though they had the unending buffet of royal banquets available. Every meal for them was a reminder that even though they were willing workers for the king, they were actually servants of the King of the universe. Other examples of items abstained from in a partial fast include: sweets or dessert fast, a juice fast, and more broadly, a news, entertainment, or phone fast. Many different partial fasts can help us discover what we are allowing to consume our limited appetites, leaving little hunger for God.

Absolute fast. To abstain for a relatively short time from all food and water. After his encounter with Jesus on the road to Damascus, Saul was not only blind, he also fasted. **"And for three days he was without sight, and neither ate nor drank."**[11] In the Old Testament we read that Ezra **"spent the night, neither eating nor drinking water, for he was mourning over the faithlessness of the exiles."**[12] And when Esther was about to take her life in her hands and go uninvited before the king, she sent these instructions to Mordecai: **"Go, gather all the Jews to be found in Susa, and hold a fast on my behalf, and do not eat or drink for three days, night or day. I and my young women will also fast as you do."**[13]

Again, an absolute fast should be taken under a doctor's advisement and only for a brief period of time.

Corporate fast. To fast in any of the above ways, but in agreement of purpose with other believers. What would happen if our church was facing a clear and present crisis? Or maybe something is wrong and we need to figure out before God what is causing the problem. If we declared a fast for the whole church, how many would participate?

The passage from Esther we just used was also an example of a corporate fast. Another time God Himself announced through His prophet Joel, **"Blow the trumpet in Zion; consecrate a fast; call a solemn assembly."**[14] In 2 Chronicles 20:3–4 the kingdom of Judah faced a powerful enemy: **"Then Jehoshaphat was afraid and set his face to seek the LORD, and proclaimed a fast throughout all Judah. And Judah assembled to seek help from the LORD; from all the cities of Judah they came to seek the LORD."** The heritage we have as believers gives us a cloud of examples of faith that practiced this spiritual discipline. Throughout history, when the going got tough for God's people, the faithful didn't just get going; they also got fasting.

In February of 1756, two-and-a-half centuries ago, the entire nation of Britain was called to a day of solemn fasting and prayer in view of the threatening invasion by the French. On February 6, 1756, John Wesley recorded in his journal:

The fast day was a glorious day; such as London scarce has ever seen. . . . Every church in the city was more than full, and a solemn seriousness sat on every face. Surely God hears prayer; and there will yet be a lengthening of our peace [and tranquillity].

The legacy of faith we pass on to new believers and those still to come to faith will be less than fully authentic if we don't take seriously our lack of hunger for God and practice more intentionally the means God has provided to keep our appetites healthy and righteous.

WHEN TO FAST

Isaiah 58 describes God's objection to the misplaced religious fasting of the people. And in Isaiah 58:3 God quotes the questions His people have asked because their careful religious practices, including fasting, haven't seemed to make any impression on Him. Then God tells them why: **"'Why have we fasted, and you see it not? Why have we humbled ourselves, and you take no knowledge of it?' Behold, in the day of your fast you seek your own pleasure, and oppress all your workers."** God continues to point out the double-mindedness of His people, fasting religiously while living lives of blatant moral disobedience. They were going through the fasting motions, but their hearts were far from God. Fasting is never a good cover for sin!

But then notice this, beginning in verse 6, God expresses His longing for a righteous kind of fasting. Here are ten answers to the question, "When should we fast?"

When we are caught in a sinful pattern

God said in Isaiah 58:6, **"Is this not the fast that I choose: to loose the bonds of wickedness ..."** When I am caught in a sinful pattern, I should fast. Authentic fasting gives God an open channel to show me how I'm held captive in bad behavior or even good behavior that's out of control. Then fasting also gives me a place or way to see God loose those bonds. Fasting reveals and breaks sinful patterns.

When we have a heavy burden

Verse 6 goes on: **"... to undo the straps of the yoke, to let the oppressed go free, and to break every yoke?"** Do you have a heavy burden you have been carrying for a long time? You're not seeing the change you need to see? Skip lunch for a whole week. Give the time you would have been spent eating to praying to God about this matter. Tell God you are seeking to pay careful attention to what He might want to tell you about your burden. Forego eating for a whole day. Start Sunday night and say, "I'm not going to eat again until Monday night or even till Tuesday morning." And let the gnawing in your stomach heighten your hunger for God.

When we are oppressed by the enemy

The end of verse 6 talks about when someone is oppressed by the enemy, **"to let the oppressed go free . . ."** I find many believers are burdened for someone in their family or in their life who's not walking with God. Names immediately flood your mind. You have prayed consistently for them. Have you fasted and prayed about the oppression, asking God to tear the veil of darkness with His light? Fasting and praying puts you in the seat where you can watch God work.

When we want to give to someone else

God goes on in Isaiah 58, **"Is it [the fast] not to share your bread with the hungry and bring the homeless poor into your house; when you see the naked, to cover him, and not to hide yourself from your own flesh?"** (v. 7). Giving that involves my doing without in order to provide for someone else is a kind of fasting. When we share "our" bread, "our" homes, "our" clothes and blankets—not the stuff we don't want or need anymore but the stuff we consider ours—that's a fasting pleasing to God. We are letting go of things we might otherwise become more dependent on than we ought. Fasting allows us to learn how to be generous not only with the surplus God provides but also with the principal God provides.

When we need to be encouraged

God's idea of fasting isn't to produce a lot of gaunt and sober-faced followers. The outcome to authentic fasting is a kind of life Jesus called *abundant*.[15] So God added through Isaiah, **"Then shall your light break forth like the dawn, and your healing shall spring up speedily; your righteousness shall go before you; the glory of the LORD shall be your rear guard"** (v. 8). The reasons for fasting may have to start out as serious resistance to the conforming power of the world around us,[16] but the results should include a lot of joy. When people see changes in us and the glory of the Lord in our lives, *they* may not know why, but *we* will realize He has left His mark on us. We will know He used fasting as His tool.

When we need an answer to prayer

"Then you shall call, and the LORD will answer; you shall cry, and he will say, 'Here I am'" (v. 9). Fasting not only clarifies our prayers, it also opens our eyes and ears to see and hear God's answers. When our hunger for God is elevated, the stuff keeping us from sensing His presence will be removed and we will know that when He says **"Here I am,"** He means it.

When we need to examine ourselves

God included some practical starting points: **"If you take away the yoke from your midst, the pointing finger, and the speaking wickedness, if you pour yourself out for the hungry and satisfy the desire of the afflicted, then shall your light rise in the darkness and your gloom be as the noonday"** (vv. 9–10). Putting burdens on others, pointing fingers at others (who said the Bible didn't have a way with words?), and speaking wickedness are all specific failures forcing us to ask, "Am I like that? Do I do that?" Sometimes we have to fast in order to get ourselves where we can consider these questions seriously.

When we need direction

Here's another outcome of fasting: **"And the LORD will guide you continually . . ."** (v. 11). Who doesn't say they want God's guidance? And yet how often do we actually demonstrate our desire by fasting and waiting attentively on God?

When we need to be spiritually restored

God not only promises guidance in Isaiah 58:11, He also points to fasting as the means He uses to restore us. **"And the LORD will . . . satisfy your desire in scorched places and make your bones strong; and you will be** like a watered garden, like a spring of water, whose waters do not fail." What a stark picture of what our lives look like to God: scorched, broken, and parched! The woman who met Jesus at the well whose story we looked at earlier in this chapter—that's what her life was like. And even though the conversation began with Jesus asking her for a drink, she quickly realized this man she was talking to was like a **"watered garden, like a spring of water, whose waters do not fail,"** and she could hardly wait to receive living water from Him.

When we need to be revived

If you've gotten to this point and are feeling hopeless; if you are thinking all this good stuff might have been true for you yesterday but not today or tomorrow, let God's truth ring in your life: **"And your ancient ruins shall be rebuilt; you shall raise up the foundations of many generations; you shall be called the repairer of the breach, the restorer of streets to dwell in"** (v.12). If you are alive, you are under renovation—you're not finished and God isn't finished with you. However "ruined" you see your life today, God can still make it possible for you to be the next generations' foundation, someone known for repairing breaches and restoring places for life to be lived authentically.

I went through this rich passage from Isaiah 58 quickly. But you could go back over the verses yourself during a time of prayer and fasting. Dig into it as I have and ask yourself the question: What does this mean? What is God promising in regard to fasting?

CONCLUSION

This is what we are going for throughout this book—authenticity! Success is measured by the world in many ways that are not necessarily authentic. I couldn't care less how big our church is. Size means nothing to me. What means everything to me is the quality of our discipleship: mine, yours, and ours. And I believe the Lord has convicted me that fasting is a neglected discipline in my life. I haven't written this as one who has great success, though I have fasted many times through the years. But I feel called back to fasting again, lest I focus on the wrong things in these disciplines of a sincere faith and make some surface adjustments, but not really get to the matters of the heart.

I want to point out to you a final Scripture: Psalm 84. Do you ever read the Scriptures and say to yourself, "I wish that I felt the way the psalmists felt about God"? Have you ever felt the gap between your faith and a writer of Scripture's faith? When the psalm says, **"A day in your courts is better than a thousand elsewhere,"**[17] does the phrase express your heart? Really? If I found out that my life was coming to an end, would I rather spend one day with the Lord's people than a thousand days—three years— anywhere else? You get three years or one day. Three years with nothing of God or one day in the house of God with God's people. Better? Your honest answer is a measure of your hunger for God.

But these worshipers weren't done: **"I would rather be a doorkeeper in the house of God than to dwell in the tents of wickedness."** Why? **"For the LORD is a sun and a shield; the LORD bestows favor and honor. No good thing does he withhold from those who walk uprightly."**[18] Those who walk uprightly before God have room in their lives for the discipline of fasting.

THE REAL THING:

Not About Coffee

I WOULD HAVE TO SAY FELLOWSHIP represents the grand, ongoing experiment of my life. I have come to see myself as a fairly relational person, but looking back, the Christian relationships I observed throughout my teen and young adult years were spectacularly unsatisfying. I was surrounded by people getting along with people and yet the last word I would use to describe those relationships would be *authentic*. The terms that seem to fit my memory of them better are: *contrived, mutually beneficial, self-serving*, but not *genuine*.

I now realize one of the driving forces behind my willingness to plant a church was the desire to see greater authenticity in relationships. Could we get it right if we started from the ground up? As one of the early leaders in our church pointed out to me, fellowship is the *result* of ministry; you don't pursue fellowship—it's a by-product. The shared and acted commitment in a great task creates a bond between people that is authentic fellowship. The greater the task, the greater the possibility exists for deep fellowship. You have the greatest potential for deepest relationships with the people you serve alongside in serving the Lord.

Having said that (and believing it), I still think there are some factors we are overlooking when we try to understand all God's Word tells us about the necessity and spiritual discipline of fellowship. The failures I see directly related to authentic fellowship led me to do my doctoral thesis on "Increasing the Incidence of Self-Disclosure of Sin among Men" several years ago. I believe disclosure is the currency of intimacy, and intimacy is the essence of fellowship. Where there is no making-yourself-known and no disclosure, fellowship cannot exist—only a caricature.

So what keeps us from fellowship? The hardest thing to disclose is personal failure, because I want people to think better of me than I know myself to really be. Disclosure is gradual, and feels risky, but that's why it can only happen where people work together long enough and close enough for life to crack the coverings and break the walls of fear we hide behind.

Fellowship creates a safe place where you can be known as you *really* are, where you don't fear rejection. I would just have to say I'm still looking for genuine fellowship among Christians. I have not found many followers of Jesus who are willing to sign up for what fellowship really involves—a true, Christ-centered, gospel-driven commitment between people that doesn't have illusions, reflecting what we see in Jesus who didn't attach Himself to man because **"He knew what was in man."**[1] He didn't have any misconceptions about people. He committed Himself to others, as He commits Himself to you and me, despite what He knows to be true of us (and He knows the *whole* story). Stanley C. Baldwin wrote a book on the church entitled *Love, Acceptance, and Commitment: Being Christian in a Non-Christian World*. In it he provides a powerful description of the quality of relationship that ought to mark Christians:

> In the Kingdom of God, we first love and then move into acquaintance. Love is a commitment and operates independently of what we feel or do not feel. We need to extend the love to everyone: I want you to know that I'm committed to you. You'll never knowingly suffer at my hands. I'll never say or do anything, knowingly to hurt you. I'll always, in every circumstance seek to help you and support you. If you're down and I can lift you up, I'll do that. Anything I

have that you need, I'll share with you; and if need be, I'll give it to you. No matter what I find out about you and no matter what happens in the future, either good or bad, my commitment to you will never change. And there's nothing you can do about it. You don't have to respond. I love you, and that's what it means.[2]

It saddens me to say I can count on the fingers of my hands those whom I personally know to be willing to engage in a multiple-decade commitment to true, biblical fellowship. Fellowship is the crucible of sanctification. God is always working to refine out qualities in your life and mine, and He has determined that this process cannot happen without our connection with each other at the fellowship level. But these days, people do esteem themselves better than others.[3] There's a low tolerance for bearing with the shortcomings in one another that must be part of authentic fellowship in a fallen world. Which is why fellowship—real, biblical relationship, as you are about to learn—is a discipline, not a scheduled event that includes coffee and pastries.

CHAPTER FIVE

THE DISCIPLINE OF FELLOWSHIP

The word *fellowship* is used many places in the New Testament. We want to start in the book of Acts because the relationships among the first followers of Jesus Christ set the bar high for every generation that has followed them. They understood and practiced the discipline for this chapter—the discipline of fellowship. Even knowing a certain level of commitment would cost many of the first Christians their lives didn't prevent them from stepping up. We can learn a lot from them!

TOP TEN THINGS THE BIBLE SAYS ABOUT FELLOWSHIP

Many people don't realize that fellowship is a discipline; not just something helpful but something *commanded*. Not just a useful exercise but a needed practice. One of the surest barometers of the quality of your Christian life is the quality of the Christian relationships in your life. When that deteriorates, you're going backwards spiritually. And the rest of the body of Christ is negatively affected, too.

Let's begin in Acts 2. God's Spirit is poured out and Peter delivers the first sermon in the postresurrection age. The church has been born and thousands are coming to Christ.

Acts 2:42 summarizes the activity of the early church when it says, **"They devoted themselves ..."**[4] Some translations say, **"They continued steadfastly ..."**[5] Both of those are good. The Greek compound term means "to be strong toward." **"They devoted themselves to the apostles' teaching and the fellowship."** Luke welcomes us into the early church and tells us to notice two characteristics: apostolic teaching and mutual fellowship.

10) Fellowship means "our common life together."

Now what is fellowship? Let's count down from #10: Fellowship means *our common life together*. Fellowship is not red punch in the church basement. Fellowship doesn't flow just because the lights are on. At Harvest we don't have a church basement, and I don't like red punch. But that's what I grew up thinking; that fellowship effortlessly happens after the service downstairs when people get around and have cheesy conversations and utter pious platitudes. Let's blow the foul whistle on that practice. What a terrible caricature of fellowship! That's not what the Bible is talking about when it says the early church was so powerful partly as a result of the kind of common life they had together.

Sometimes I hear people say, "We're having Bill and Sheila over after church. We'll watch the Bears' game and have some fellowship." Well, maybe you will; maybe you won't. Watching the Bears' game is fun. That's not fellowship. Now I'm all in favor of fun. There's nothing wrong with enjoying each other's company, but that's not fellowship, so let's not confuse the two. Fellowship is something a lot deeper and more substantive than fun.

The Greek word Luke uses for *fellowship* is *koinonia. Koinonia* is sometimes translated in the English New Testament *participation*. The word is also translated *partnership, sharing, communion,* or this summary word, *fellowship.*

Here is a longer and more precise definition: fellowship is a relationship between individuals that involves (this is key) active participation (it's what we share) in a common interest. As a result of our participation in the common interest, we have a residual interest in one another. To say it again simply, fellowship is our common life together.

Now Harvest Bible Chapel currently meets on six campuses in sixteen services each weekend. I only attend three services; most of the members only attend one. But we are one church in several locations bound together by a common purpose. And as we engage in that common purpose, the relationships that are the result of full participation generate fellowship.

I want you to get a sense of the power in the fellowship of a church. It spans time and space. I treasure a black-and-white photograph of a church building in Canada called Central Baptist Church in London, Ontario. That's the church I grew up in and where I spent, for the most part, the first twenty years of my life. But my family has been connected for a lot longer.

Written on the back of the picture are notes about our family history. My paternal grandparents were married in this church in 1935. It's where my mom and dad were married in 1956. My paternal grandmother, who prayed so much for me—her funeral was in that building in August 2001. My mother was saved in this church in 1952. I met Christ under that roof in 1967 and so did my wife, Kathy, in 1978. All of my brothers committed their lives to Christ in this building. Most of my family was baptized in this church. So was Kathy's mom. A remarkable record of historic heritage events is handwritten on the back of that photograph. I preached the first sermon I ever preached in that church in March of 1978. Then I walked to the front of the sanctuary, knelt down, and gave my life to the Lord for full-time ministry on November 12, 1979.

In preparing this chapter I was reviewing all of the things that had been recorded on that thick, yellowed paper. I've glanced at both sides of this photograph many times. It hangs in our home. But it wasn't until recently that something obvious stood out to me: every notation on the back of that picture is in my mother's handwriting. One significant event she couldn't write down was her own funeral at this same church just a couple years ago. So many lives and so much history represented by one photograph.

Now that is an awesome thing: the power of one church. The only reason Kathy and I are still in our present location is because God called us to remember and replicate in another place what we experienced in the life of that congregation. What holds all of our history together is the Spirit of God working through the Word of God and our service to God to bind us together in love toward one another. Don't miss the meaning of true fellowship: *our common life together.*

9) Fellowship was a high priority in the early church.

Acts 2:42 confirms fellowship was a high priority in the early church. I mean, when you read the verse, you might say to yourself, **"And they devoted themselves to the apostles' teaching and . . ."** What will be next? Well, surely it must be Bible study or prayer, for goodness sakes, or they devoted themselves to evangelism. I think a lot of people have a sense that somehow this relationship stuff between us is sort of a nice add-on, maybe a little whipped topping on the dessert of the Christian life—but not a main thing or the second thing. Incorrect! Fellowship *is* the second thing Luke mentions.

Some people reading this are trying to live the Christian life on their own. You may attend church, come in and out, but you're not really connected. You're not in the life of the church, in community with other people, or actively engaging in common life together. You're not acting like those first Christians. Fellowship was a high priority in the early church. It's the second characteristic of their community.

Let's go over five basic reasons people give for *not* devoting themselves to the fellowship. I've got another survey for you here similar to the one in the last chapter:

The Fifth Basic Reason for Not Fellowshipping

1   XXXXXXXXXXXXXXXXXX
2   XXXXXXXXXXXXXXXXXX
3   XXXXXXXXXXXXXXXXXX
4   XXXXXXXXXXXXXXXXXX
5   TOO BUSY

Don't people often say this? They shrug their shoulders and explain, "I'd like to spend time fellowshipping, connecting, belonging, and the residual by-product of serving, but I've got a lot going on in my life." Really?! Does it satisfy you to see your Christian experience has become so much like a desert because you think you're too busy for what is not optional—authentic fellowship?

The schedule is just a smoke screen for other issues that show up later. Here's one:

Fourth Basic Reason for Not Fellowshipping

1   XXXXXXXXXXXXXXXXXX
2   XXXXXXXXXXXXXXXXXX
3   XXXXXXXXXXXXXXXXXX
4   **FEAR**
5   TOO BUSY

People are afraid. "I . . . I . . . I . . . I don't know if I want people to know me. I don't think I'm as good a Christian as some of these other people." That's perception. The truth is, **"We all stumble in many ways."**[6] The apostle Paul made the shared territory even broader: **"No temptation has overtaken you that is not common to man."**[7] At least one of us knows what it is for you to struggle in certain regards. Don't allow yourself the luxury of imagining no one has the struggles like you have. Among all of us, some of us have dealt with the exact thing you're facing. You don't need to be afraid to make yourself known. "But I really got my feelings hurt. I was involved in another church some time ago. And I was so disappointed. I was so injured by the people and I'm afraid of the hurt happening again."

In fact, the number three answer combines past experiences with fear: Third Basic Reason for Not Fellowshipping

1   XXXXXXXXXXXXXXXXX
2   XXXXXXXXXXXXXXXXX
3   NO TRUST
4   FEAR
5.   TOO BUSY

"I—I can't trust people. I can't let people get close to me again. I . . . I . . ." Listen. I'm sorry for what happened to you. I don't minimize it in any way. But I would plead with you to give yourself and the body of a good church another chance. Maybe you *have* been deeply wounded. But the thing you need is not to hide from the pain. Staying away won't promote healing. The thing you need is to let some precious people in a Christ-centered church get their arms around you. You can be cautious, but let them love on you. Allow other believers to care for you. Look for ways to care for them. Fellowship is always both ways, not one way. Christians want to enter into meaningful fellowship with each other. No one wants a church to be merely a place for you to attend with no strings attached. The language is archaic but our forefathers were on to something when they sang, "Blest be the ties that bind."

I'm sorry those things happened that left you wounded, hurt, and angry. But you can't live your whole life on the past. Authentic fellowship is the answer.

Second Basic Reason for Not Fellowshipping

1   XXXXXXXXXXXXXXXXX
2   DON'T NEED IT
3   NO TRUST
4   FEAR
5   TOO BUSY

You really think you don't need fellowship? Wrong! The spiritual poverty you feel, the isolation you sense, and the battles you go through just to do some of the basic things of the Christian life should be convincing clues; the Christian life is not a solo sport. You weren't saved to go it alone. If fellowship was number two on early Christians' list, who are we to think we can get along without their kind of genuine connectedness?

In many ways, the first reason given for avoiding fellowship, when it is finally revealed, combines the effects of all the above:

First Basic Reason for Not Fellowshipping

1   SECRETS

2   DON'T NEED IT

3   NO TRUST

4   FEAR

5.   TOO BUSY

There it is. "Things aren't going very well for me. And I'm afraid if I let people get too close, they're going to find some stuff out about me. They're going to see the contents aren't the same as the cover." All right; true enough. I hear the hesitation to disclose. But deep in your heart of hearts, do you envision the rest of your life struggling with that painful or shameful secret, whatever it is? I don't know of a better place than fellowship to bring those kinds of things into the light. Because I'm telling you, self-disclosure is all over the place in authentic fellowship. The church Christ died for is not a pretend gathering. It is a not a put-on-a-front group. Jesus never meant His followers to participate in a pose, act-like-everything-is-great church. This is a place to bring it forward; get it out, and get it gone.

> **IF YOU DON'T HAVE A STRONG FELLOWSHIP FACTOR IN YOUR CHRISTIAN LIFE, IT'S NOT AUTHENTIC.**

I'm not saying that "church" on the sign outside automatically means authentic fellowship inside the walls. Once you decide to engage or re-engage, do some church homework. Get a copy of the bulletin. Check out the church website. Call one of the pastors. Everything people struggle with (including you) is being addressed by some church near where you live. You find *that* group of people. Get with them. It will be a safe place for you to bring out *your* secret and get to a better place. Here's the takeaway point: if you don't have a strong fellowship factor in your Christian life, it's not authentic.

8) Fellowship is for believers only.

Did you know that? Fellowship as the Bible talks about it is only for Christians. I don't appreciate it when people use our word. Fellowship is not friendship. Friendship is important, but fellowship is deeper than that. Second Corinthians 6:14 says, **"Do not be unequally yoked with unbelievers . . ."** Do you know what *yoked* means? The picture is two oxen about the same size with the same strength, harnessed so they work as one. When you and your plow head down the field with them, they're going to cut a straight furrow. But what if you get an unequally yoked team? You have an ox on one side and beaver on the other side. That's not going very good! That plow will be all over the field. You've got to have matched animals in the same yoke.

Here's the picture again with its application: **"Do not be unequally yoked with unbelievers. For what partnership has righteousness with lawlessness?"** Don't have a believer on one side who is righteous through faith in Christ and an unbeliever who is still under the law on the other side. Don't have a person who is in the light on one slot of the yoke and a person who's in the darkness on the other slot. You say, "Man. When you described that ox and beaver pair, that seemed so weird." Or are they actually a better combination than a person in the light and a person in the darkness trying to partner?

You may be in a mixed-match marriage like the ox and beaver because you didn't obey this verse. Or you are in a strained marriage now because though you started as equally matched unbelievers, one of you has come to know Christ and your spouse hasn't come along yet. God may still show a lot of grace to people in those situations. Maybe she or he is going to come to Christ very soon. But don't choose an unequal yoke because you think God's warning isn't true. Don't ever assume that just because you're "in love," you can ignore what God clearly says.

Now a primary application of that principle when I was growing up was to dating relationships. Don't start dating and falling in love with someone who isn't a believer. But the unequal yoke rule can also apply to other areas. Don't go into business with someone who doesn't love the Lord and obey God's Word like you do. I've heard too many sad stories about business plans that had such great potential except they involved the "little" matter of a partnership with a really nice and smart unbeliever. Those unequal yokes plowed lives into disaster.

However, I think a primary application of equal yoking has to do with *friendship*. Hear me. Your closest friendships should not be with unbelievers. Now, should we have friendships with unbelievers? Yes. Absolutely. We should reach out to people and love them and show them the love of Christ. But we should *not* be getting our primary connection needs met by people who do not know and love the Lord. Our closest relationships, our life-giving friendships, should be with people who know and love Jesus Christ like we do.

Now it is hard for some people to appreciate when we say fellowship is for believers only. You might be thinking, "Well, my non-Christian friends and I got a good thing going on. We have our little circle over here. And I would feel bad if anyone was left out." Here's the problem. In order for us to make our relationships as deep as they can be, we cannot accommodate someone who doesn't know and love the Lord. If you're reading this as someone who hasn't given their life to Christ yet, I'm glad you're here. I want to welcome you in and encourage you along the journey. But you need to realize this. In order for us to make our relationships into something that would work for a nonbeliever, we have to reduce our interaction to almost nothing! And we can't settle for surface limitations in conversation. Fellowship is too important to sacrifice for casual friendship. Conversely, by the way, followers of Jesus discover the amazing dynamic of meeting another believer for the first time, perhaps even from another culture, and within moments you are talking about the deepest matters of life as if you've known each other for years. Having Christ in common closes a lot of distance between people. So let's embrace the reality: real, meaningful fellowship is for believers only.

7) Fellowship centers on our common relationship to Christ.

First Corinthians 1:9 says, **"God is faithful, by whom you were called into the fellowship of his Son, Jesus Christ our Lord."** You see, our primary fellowship is with Jesus Christ. And then the residual fellowship is the relationship we have with other people who share the connection with Christ. You say, "Well, James, I feel it's going a lot better with me and the Lord than it is with me and other Christians." Sometimes that's because we bring secular ways of relating into our Christian relationships.

Let me give you three levels of conversation. I encourage you to take your relationships with all Christians as deep as you possibly can. Here is the first level of relationship:

Surface Level

That's where you talk about stuff like weather. "You know, that snowstorm was something, wasn't it? *That* was really coming down. We haven't had a whiteout like that since . . . the last time the media scared us to death!" I was actually very happy to be alive after the last Chicago blizzard. I was fairly sure digging out the drifts would be the end for me. But talking about it is low-risk, low-reward interaction.

Surface conversation doesn't move beyond sports and mundane experiences. "How 'bout them Bears?" And "Wow! We went to a great restaurant." Unfortunately this is what passes for fellowship in a lot of people's minds. This kind of interaction doesn't even show up on the fellowship meter! Let's go to the next level.

Personal Level

This doesn't have to involve another Christian to have a conversation where you talk about someone's health or career. "We've been praying for you. How's it going with your son?" That's personal and expresses care. Some people would say it's neighborly, or decent to show a level of interest in others. Sharing what Jesus means to you is the ultimate in personal interaction. Before conversations reach the next and deepest level, they usually begin at the personal level. But if they *stay* there, that's not fellowship, either.

Spiritual Level

Here's what you're going for with other believers. This is where fellowship really begins; where you're having conversations with them that you can't have with anybody else. Now this is where you're praying together and you're talking about what ultimately matters. When you share Jesus with someone at the personal level and God's Spirit prompts them to respond to Him, you not only move immediately to the spiritual level, you also begin to experience fellowship.

Kathy and I were away recently with a couple in our church who we've known for a long time. And we had some precious fellowship. We didn't just talk about the weather. We didn't just converse about our health or our family. We prayed. And we talked about our relationship with the Lord—I mean *talked*! I am telling you, you know what it's like to go out for dinner with another believer but you don't talk about anything different than you would with the guy across the office at work? How disappointing! How shallow! How secondary! What a failure to make use of the incredible opportunity we have. Yes, we could touch on the surface subjects. Surely we can talk about personal things. But always try to get it to level 3. In fact, here are some decisions that will help you to get it to the spiritual level:

Don't rush.

You know the guy who comes up to you and opens with, "Hey! Let me tell you what I got out of the Bible this week, and when I'm done, you can tell me how it's going with one of the private sins in your life?" It's like you just got on the elevator and someone hit the express button to level 3, but it feels like the cable broke and you're plunging toward the basement!

You're like, "Whoa! Whoa! What's your name again?" Don't rush, friend. Can we just ease into this a little bit? Do you have any style to go with your intensity? Don't drag or push people deeper when you haven't even connected with them yet!

Go first.

Rather than saying to somebody, "Hey! How's your quiet time going? Are you getting victory over the sin you mentioned?" why don't you start? Disclose before you ask someone else to disclose. Don't invite people to go to a level where you haven't gone yourself. "It's great to see you because I've wanted to tell you about how I'm doing with the Lord."

Be specific.

Down with Christian platitudes and clichés in our conversations with other believers. There is nothing worse than the backslapping Christian guy who's always like, "Hey, brother! You know, God is on the throne. And He owns the cattle on a thousand hills!" And da da-da da-da.

You're thinking, "What?! What are you talking about, man? Who talks like that? Why don't you get real, man? Why don't you get Pastor James's sermon series on *Authentic* and memorize it." Enough with spiritual slogans dropped on other believers. How about genuine, heartfelt, compassionate conversation?

I had a great moment when Kathy and I were with the couple I mentioned above. The wife, over dinner, brought up something that Kathy and I had told her about six or eight months ago that was a burden to us. She waited until the right time in the conversation, then she gently asked, "How's that going? I've been praying for you about it since you told me."

I said, "Wow! That is so amazing that you've been thinking about that."

And she answered, "Well, I care."

Yeah, yeah, you do, I thought. That's stunning and comforting! That's what we're going for. And nobody can do it for you like another follower of Jesus Christ. God help all of us to deepen the level of our interaction with one another. Fellowship centers on our common relationship with Christ.

6) Fellowship involves sharing what I have.

Authentic fellowship will require you to keep a personal inventory. What do you have? How has God equipped you as a person to function with other people? Start down the list: "I have time. I have wisdom. I have compassion. I have resources. I have experience. I have . . ." Whatever you have—that's your inventory.

While writing to the Corinthians, Paul reminded them what a good example the Macedonians were about giving. He says, **"We want you to know, brothers, about the grace of God that has been given among the churches of Macedonia . . ."**[8] Here's what was going on. Because of persecution and a regional famine, some of the Jewish Christians in Jerusalem were starving. I mean *starving*, starving. So some of the churches in Asia Minor took up offerings to send relief to fellow believers in Jerusalem. But amazingly, some of the people who gave really didn't have—humanly speaking—very much to give. Paul went on to describe the grace God was pouring out through the young churches in Macedonia:

> **For in a severe test of affliction, their abundance of joy and their extreme poverty have overflowed in a wealth of generosity on their part. For they gave according to their means, as I can testify** (So it wasn't the biggest gifts, but it may have been the biggest sacrifice.), **and beyond their means, of their own free will, begging us earnestly for the favor of taking part in the relief of the saints.**[9]

"Oh please let us give! Oh please, here's our offering."

"Well, you all aren't doing so well yourselves."

"No, no, no! We'll find a way. We *want* to give!"

That's the heart of fellowship right there. On the outside it may look like it's all about a **"severe test of affliction"** and **"extreme poverty,"** but authentic fellowship turns those hardships into **"abundance of joy"** and an overflowing **"wealth of generosity."**

You know, it happened again to me this week. I was speaking at a conference down in St. Louis. And a pastor asked, "How is it the people at Harvest give the way they do?"

I said, "Well, it's not because the church is full of wealthy people, I can tell you that. Because it isn't. I don't know what individual people give, but I'm told our needs are not met by large gifts. They are met by many faithful, sacrificial gifts." Believers today who act like the Macedonians of Paul's day need to be commended for the way they practice generous fellowship.

I wonder if you are part of that kind of fellowship. Join the team because what you offer will be used to plant more churches and proclaim the kingdom of Christ. If you *are* a part of generous giving, I challenge you that it's not just simply about writing a check. It's giving ourselves and caring for one another and loving one another. This is an expression of fellowship in which we can always grow.

Don't you want your church to be a compelling testimony of the power of the gospel in the way the people love and care for one another? Every time you write a note. Your care in making a meal and taking it over to someone who's hurting. Each time you drop by the hospital. When you seek someone out about something you heard in small group. Every time you reach out to someone standing in the lobby who looks like they're alone and you say, "Hey, I care for you." All of these are fellowship in motion, sharing what you have.

Those who walk in, walk out, walk in, walk out, but never enter into relationships are missing out on a central aspect of what it means to be in Christ—fellowship with other believers. Find a way to get connected and give yourself, sharing what you have with Christ with other people. Fellowship is a powerful thing! And we all need it.

5) Fellowship is about partnership in ministry.

By the time Luke wrote this history of the early church in Acts, lots of practices and relationships had gotten settled. To get an early report from the front lines, we can turn to Galatians, the first letter Paul wrote, talking about his testimony and recounting the way he was brought into the church after being the lead persecutor of believers. Eventually, he met with the leaders of the church, men he previously had on his will-kill list. Talk about a meeting with potential for distrust! In Galatians 2:9 Paul wrote, **"and when James and Cephas and John, who seemed to be pillars…"** These were the main leaders in the church: James (Jesus' half brother), Peter (whose name was also Cephas), and John. When they **"perceived the grace that was given to me,"** Paul said. In other words, "When they figured out that I was saved," **"they gave the right hand of fellowship to Barnabas and me."**

Try to imagine this scene. Barnabas and Paul arrive in Jerusalem and ask to meet with the leaders of the church. Galatians 1:19–23 tells us that earlier in his new life of following Jesus, Paul had met with Peter and James briefly, but then had immediately embarked on missionary work. But the word got around in Judea that something had happened to the dreaded Saul. **"They only were hearing it said, 'He who used to persecute us is now preaching the faith he once tried to destroy.' And they glorified God because of me."**[10] Now it's more than a decade later and Paul has been out among the Gentiles, planting churches. He wasn't present when Jesus gave the Great Commission in Matthew 28:19–20, but Paul has been out doing it for years. He's coming to explain **"the gospel that I proclaim among the Gentiles, in order to make sure I was not running or had not run in vain."**[11] This tells us a lot about Paul's attitude. He wasn't showing up as the I'm-out-there-winning-the-world-what-have-*you*-guys-done guy. He was coming to submit his message to the leadership of the church for confirmation.

But what about the "pillars" in Jerusalem? Were they threatened by Paul's success? Were they eager to poke holes in his theology and insist on his obedience? Would they even acknowledge his ministry? I mean, here are Peter and John, two of the Towering Twelve! Then there was James, Jesus' brother who believed after the resurrection and became a force in the early church. By comparison, Paul and Barnabas were newcomers and still small fish in the pond. How would the meeting go? Would the egos clash?

The leaders saw something in Paul he called **"the grace that was given to me."**[12] That wasn't "when they saw what a powerful preacher I had become," or "when they realized how many people had come to faith through me"—no, it was a grace, the grace and presence of Jesus in Paul's life that was apparent to Peter, James, and John. And they didn't hesitate. It was the midfield handshake, hugs, and welcome taken up a big notch. They reached out and said, "Come on in now. We're all in this together with Christ. We are glad you are here. You didn't come a day late."

Their **"right hand of fellowship"** was authentic and it came with a purpose, **"...that we should go to the Gentiles."**[13] Paul and Barnabas were welcomed in, in order to be sent out. You are in your fellowship for a reason. You are part of your church for a purpose; and it can't begin to really happen until you join with others in fellowship; and participate with them in missions so that others can come to know Jesus Christ. Fellowship is about partnership in ministry!

4) Fellowship requires commitment.

As he did at the beginning of most of his letters, Paul thanked God for the Philippian Christians: **"Because of your partnership** (or **fellowship;** it's the same word) **in the gospel from the first day until now."**[14]

> **THERE ARE NO ENDURING RELATIONSHIPS WITHOUT FORGIVENESS.**

Notice that phrase **"from the first day until now."** Starting in a relationship is easy; continuing in relationship is difficult. It's one thing to say, "I will commit to you." It's another to say, even when life has had its way, "I'll stay committed to you."

Almost every weekend at Harvest, I notice Bill and Nadine Martin sitting somewhere in the congregation. They were part of the original eighteen people who started this church over twenty-five years ago. I could fill books with the stories of the things that we've experienced and have had to overcome together. But much of it is our shared history together, not for sharing with anyone else.

A lot has happened in a quarter century. But every few months, every few years, something comes up that we have to overcome all over again in order to keep loving and serving. It's not easy to be in one church for years and decades. Authentic fellowship makes it possible.

There are no enduring relationships without forgiveness. We all disappoint one another in many ways. But if we're going for authenticity in Christ, we're going to have to keep on with our commitment. Paul thanked God and the Philippians for their fellowship in the gospel from the first day until now. The greater glory goes to Jesus Christ—not when we take our marbles and go home because something didn't work out the way we wanted it. The greater glory goes to Jesus Christ when we pursue and persevere in relationship in spite of the shortcomings that we see in one another. Because it's not about you. And it's not about me. It's about growing in love together for the glory of God. And that has always required commitment.

Here are five blows that break down commitment:

***Entitlement* can prevent or destroy commitment.** When you come to church to get, get, get without much thought about giving. A sense of entitlement thinks, "Well, I'm giving them my presence—I'm here. That's my part; their part is to meet my needs." Now let's be honest with ourselves, the church of Jesus Christ is a place where we all get, where we *all* receive. I pray Harvest Bible Chapel will be a place for people to get a lot. I'm certainly giving with a goal to make sure those with whom I've been entrusted will richly receive. And every time the church is gathered, many are giving with the intention that others would benefit from their service. But if you never cross the bridge from "what-I-get" to "what-I-can-give," your church will become for you increasingly unsatisfactory. Church is a place to receive at the outset, but quickly it needs to also become a place to give.

I bumped into a man in the hallway recently between services. I haven't talked to him personally for probably four years. He was helpfully serving people. I gave him a big hug. We caught up with each other for a few moments, but both of us had duties to carry out. Just seeing him at his post was an encouragement to me. We have all of eternity to talk! This is our opportunity to make a difference, to shine a light in a dark world. Find a job and do it—forever—until Christ returns. Roll up your sleeves and get to work. Selfless service requires commitment.

Entitlement breaks commitment. God protect me from an entitled heart. "I deserve to get. I must have. I can't continue if I don't receive." There's no room in that heart for fellowship.

Superiority also prevents or destroys commitment. You took a seminar or read a book and you know you learned something. You can hardly wait to pass it on. People are going to be stunned. Proverbs 3:7 (NKJV) says (I love this verse because I love stuff that's clear. How clear is this?), **"Do not be wise in your own eyes."** It means more than just the danger of having too high a view of our own wisdom; it's also sensing the danger in the "I's" (What *I* think, what *I* want, what *I* say) as the ultimate measure of wisdom. Don't think your opinion is so worthy you would break fellowship with someone because they don't see a matter the same way.

I was up early this morning, and I wrote what I hope was a very loving email to a wonderful couple in our church who contacted me with a question about a message I gave recently. Their tone was so gracious and kind. I tried to match those qualities because the point of disagreement is so unimportant compared to our common life together. And I know they will receive it as that.

But if you are wise in your own eyes, that's not going anywhere good. Both entitlement and superiority stifle fellowship. But here's another danger:

Agenda-Driven Participation **can prevent or destroy commitment.**
These come in several predictable packages that show up frequently in
church.

Doctrinal Agendas

I'm sorry to tell you that people come to churches with a doctrinal agenda. Some arrive with a position staked out and armed to
defend it at any cost. "I'm going to push what I believe over here at
Harvest. What a great place for me to advance my particular convictions." Bad plan! We have a low tolerance for personal agendas
here. Trust me—we're going to find a trouble spot and root it out
in a hurry. We don't let people hijack Harvest for their biblical
preferences.

Instead, we use a time-honored summary of the way Christian
commitment works in the body of Christ:

On the majors? Conviction.

On the minors? Tolerance.

In all things? Love.

Yes, on the central doctrines of the Christian faith, we stand with
the core of followers of Jesus across the centuries to assert (among
other truths) the irreplaceable role of the Word of God and the
life-changing message of the gospel of Jesus Christ. There's no
room for compromise in these convictions. But we also recognize
there are many areas of less important, personal preferences,
and when it comes to those, we seek to practice biblical tolerance. Insisting on perfect agreement on every point, no matter
how trivial, creates an environment where commitment simply
can't survive. We find taught in Scripture and repeatedly mod-
eled throughout church history a command to love always, in all
things, even when we disagree.

So on the majors—conviction; on the minors—tolerance; and
in all things—love. That's what we say when responding to those
who want to inject a personal theological agenda or preference

into our corporate life. God help us to do that even more faithfully.

Business Agendas

Some agendas aren't doctrinal; they are just business. I can't tell you how many people see the church as little more than a target for their multilevel something-or-other. Instead of fellow believers gathering to worship God and be instructed by Him, they only see a target-rich environment of potential customers. To which we say, "Not here! Do not come to church to sell things. We only have one product here and it's a Person—and He's free!"

So thank God for your business. I pray that the Lord will prosper you in your work, whatever it is in every respect. Don't bring it to church, okay?

Ministry Agendas

How about this awkward development? Some people have a ministry agenda. There are many people in our church who have wonderful ministries. But I thank God for those who don't jam their ministry agenda into the life of the church. We want to always encourage personal ministry, but not at the expense of what God wants to do in His church at large. God may have led you to a specific need or group of people, but trying to make your calling into the calling for the whole church is going to create problems. We hope that association with Harvest blesses people's ministries, but those particular concerns can't become the central focus of the church.

All these different agendas may have a good purpose, but when they are brought into the church, they break commitment to fellowship. Beyond these, two other personal traits seriously limit the experience and reality of fellowship in the church.

Aloofness

Some people are aloof in their approach to life in the church. When I'm preaching, I can spot them in the seats. They *never* cross the line between the front section and the back section of the sanctuary. They keep their distance from the action. They hang on the fringes of a congregation for months or years. Internally, these people are spectacularly dissatisfied at the quality of their Christian relationships. But it doesn't seem to occur to them to come forward. They may be *in* church, but they're never *of* church. They attend; they don't really participate. They avoid the very choices that would bring them into fellowship. There are seven or eight thousand adults and young people in small groups in our church. What a phenomenal effort is under way to involve people in meaningful, shepherding, mutually caring relationships.

You say, "Well, yeah, we tried a small group. It didn't go that well."

Try again. Maybe you had that weird "platitude guy" in your small group! We're trying to help him, too. Try another small group and give some people an opportunity. I don't know of a better place anywhere in the world than a healthy small group to experience the kind of loving and caring Jesus wants us to practice with each other. Step forward and participate.

Your step doesn't have to be a big one. Fill out a visitor card or register at your church—someone reads those! Write, "I'd like to participate more fully in this church. Please call me." Or write down a prayer request.

At Harvest, we track attendance on every person. We have part-time staff on all of our campuses, wonderful people who enter every person's attendance into a computer program every week. So if you miss for three weeks? I don't know the exact schedule, but if you're absent for a while, you get a letter. And if you miss more weeks, you get a phone call. And if you miss even longer? That's never happened, okay? Eventually, someone comes to find you.

You're thinking, "WHAT?! Why would you go to all that effort?"

Here's what we've learned. The number one complaint of people who don't go to church anymore? "Nobody called me. I didn't show up and no one noticed."

Here's a second thing we've learned: People who wipe out spiritually; who flip upside down in a ditch; or whose lives are coming apart at the seams? They don't call the church and say, "Hey, I just want you to know. I am off track big-time. I'm going downhill and picking up speed." We *never* get that call. So unless we keep track of people and go find them when they're hurting, struggling, stumbling, falling—the very things someone did for us at points in our lives—we won't be able to meet those needs.

We have never said to someone, "You *have* to fill out an attendance card." But we want them to know that when they write down their name, they are saying, "I want to be cared for."

Here's the reality. Every week at Harvest we have hundreds of people who have been attending for many months and years and they're not yet committed to fellowship with us. They lose and so do we. There is such power in commitment. If you want to have an authentic faith, you can't afford to be aloof.

And here's the last reason of five things that break commitment to fellowship.

Injury prevents or destroys commitment. You just get your feelings hurt (or you got them hurt). "I got hurt. I got hurt. I got hurt." My mom used to quote the following poem all the time—

I've asked the Lord to take from me,

The supersensitivity.

That robs the soul of joy and peace,

And causes fellowship to cease.

I can remember her saying this about people who lose fellowship because they got offended or wounded by others. What a great thing to pray! "Hey, Lord. Don't let me be so sensitive. God, when I get my feelings hurt, keep me from turning away. I don't want to give up on people You bring into my life."

All of this to make the point that fellowship requires commitment.

Neither fellowship nor commitment is ever entirely risk free. But we can't really have one without the other.

Kathy and I have never been more committed to nor more joyful in our participation in the life of the church we serve. And I challenge you to recommit to your church. Make the commitment to fellowship even though you know that the relationship will include hurts sometimes.

3) Fellowship hurts sometimes.

Fellowship does hurt sometimes. And that's why, in Philippians 3:10, Paul wrote, **"That I may know him (Jesus) and the power of his resurrection, and may share his sufferings . . ."** (*share in* is the term *koinonia* most often translated *fellowship*). So the verse literally says, **"That I may know him (Jesus) and the power of his resurrection and the fellowship of his sufferings . . ."**[15] What is the fellowship of Jesus' suffering? Do you know what it is?

Some people think, "Well, when I realize how much Jesus suffered for my sins, I'm thankful." Incorrect. The fellowship of His sufferings is the relational connection born of your mutual experience. Now many people experience suffering. People suffer financial loss, health problems, and family breakup. None of those hardships are the fellowship of His suffering.

Here's the gospel—don't miss this—Jesus Christ paid the debt for our sin. He took upon Himself the punishment for your sin and mine. Question: Did He deserve that? (Answer? No!) But did He take it; accept it freely? (Yes!) And I experience the fellowship of His suffering when I accept (as He did) a pain I do not deserve. In those moments, I'm sensing firsthand, in a small way, what Jesus went through.

Twenty-three years ago I didn't know *any*thing about the fellowship of His suffering. But in pastoring and leading a church, you frequently experience the injury of receiving something unfair or undeserved. Believe me, I've done plenty things where I deserved what I got. But in addition to my own failings, there is the pain of misunderstanding, betrayal, and rejection—all the things Christ experienced. I trust that in some way you can relate in your own life. When you embrace unmerited suffering and don't speak out in your own defense or go to war over things you can handle with His grace, when you absorb it for the sake of others, you are participating in the fellowship of Jesus' sufferings. This lesson affects parents, employers, small group members, and any Christian involved in committed relationships. When you absorb the injury for the sake of others, you know Jesus in a new and deeper way. You know Him in the fellowship of His suffering. He took what He did not deserve. And when we do the same, we confirm the fact that fellowship includes pain.

2) Fellowship requires honesty.

First John 1:6–9 presents such a good picture of the requirement of honesty in fellowship:

If we say we have fellowship with him while we walk in darkness, we lie and not practice the truth. But if we walk in the light, as he is in the light, we have fellowship with one another, and the blood of Jesus his Son cleanses us from all sin. If we say we have no sin, we deceive ourselves, and the truth is not in us. If we confess our sins, he is faithful and just to forgive us our sins and to cleanse us from all unrighteousness.

This is the heart of genuine fellowship. Authenticity requires honesty—not putting on a mask; not coming to church and acting okay when I'm not; instead weeping with those who weep, rejoicing with those who rejoice, bearing one another's burdens, and so fulfill the law of Christ.[16] God forbid that any church would ever become a place of pretense. Verse 7 makes this so clear. When we walk with Jesus, who is the light, we end up having real fellowship with each other. Sin isn't denied or ignored; it's cleansed and removed: **"But if we walk in the light, as he is in the light, we have fellowship with one another, and the blood of Jesus his Son cleanses us from all sin."**

And lastly,

1) Fellowship produces unity.

A commitment to fellowship is a commitment to unity. You can review the example of Christ in Philippians 2:1–5, where the ESV has ***participation in the Spirit*** to translate *koinonia* or ***fellowship in the Spirit***. But in Ephesians 4:3 we find this description of those who are walking in a manner worthy of their calling in Christ.[17] They are **"eager to maintain the unity of the Spirit in the bond of peace."** God's Spirit wants His church to be unified. Do you understand His intention? Are you walking in that truth? God's Spirit wants us to love and forgive and forbear with one another. The **"bond of peace"** is what God's Spirit is going for in our church, desiring we would stay together and work together. And **"unity of the Spirit"** is going to require all the aspects of authentic fellowship we talked about in this chapter. Fellowship may generate lots of different experiences, but ultimately it is a spiritual discipline in which we deliberately engage.

THE REAL THING:

Keep Moving

I HAVE FOUND THERE ARE certain predictable trajectories our lives can take once we become followers of Jesus Christ. The discipline of serving Him has a direct and noticeable effect on the degree to which personal, spiritual growth plateaus or continues upward throughout a person's life this side of eternity. Service is the day-to-day proving ground of how we are internalizing what Christ has done for us and our understanding of how He wants us to relate to other people.

Very early in my walk with Christ, the student pastor in our church began to take me with him on visits with other students. These were encouragement visits and often focused on praying with people. Not a lot was required of me, but the experiences of involvement in direct ministry simply whet my appetite for more. After a while I was encouraged to lead Bible studies, and then Kathy and I, before we were married, served together in a bus ministry. We piled fifty or sixty kids in a bus and brought them to Sunday school, unknowingly breaking every transport code on the books, but eager to make it possible for children in the neighborhood to find Christ. Precariously perched in the front with my guitar, I led the kids in song on the way to church. And on Saturdays, we were often in the homes of those kids, meeting their parents and praying with the family.

Eventually, the first funeral I ever did, at the age of twenty-three, was for a little girl from our bus ministry, plunging me pretty deep into the heartbreaking aspects of serving people on behalf of Christ. I now realize with gratitude that those who watched over my early spiritual development were wise enough to keep opening new doors of responsibility and opportunity for ministry that confirmed my growth and pushed me further in serving Christ.

If you gave me fifty young people today and told me my task was to get them excited about Jesus, I wouldn't sit them down for a Bible study. I'd put them to work serving the Lord. Certainly responsibilities equal to their level of maturity, but genuine serving Christ and others in ways that matter. Children and, for that matter, families ministering together in places like nursing homes are seeds of real ministry capable of bearing great fruit later on. Nothing inflames your passion for the kingdom like rolling up your sleeves and getting involved yourself. I don't really know any people in effective ministry who began as a result of something they learned; they all grew into ministry as a result of what they saw God do with their efforts on behalf of others. Even at a young age, ministry is the experience of offering your little gift of five loaves and two fishes and seeing God multiply it into so much more.

Yes, I think kids should be in Bible study, but their attention and interest will be ratcheted up to a different level when they come to it with the needs and problems of the world and their neighbors fresh on their minds. Nothing drives you to open God's Word like a real person asking you hard questions about your faith. The discipline of serving is an absolute accelerant in the process of spiritual formation.

CHAPTER SIX

THE DISCIPLINE OF SERVICE

I want to be authentic. And I trust if you've read to this point in the book, your own fires of authenticity have been stoked. You've rejected the video fireplace and the fake cellophane flames blown by a fan—you want the hot coals and crackling reality of a genuine relationship with Christ, fueled by the Holy Spirit. You're not going to settle for a cheap knockoff Christian life but are going for the life God planned and wants to empower in you!

I don't know how much longer I'm going to be in this world. And I don't want to get to the finish line with a bunch of unfinished stuff God wanted to do in my life. I don't want to waste time on the minimum requirements and the "I'll figure it out later" approach to living for God. I want to be what God wants me to be *now*. And I want to be real, genuine, and sincere. I don't want to look the part; I don't want to go through the motions. I want to *have it*—authentic faith.

I think a lot of people feel the longing for spiritual authenticity. I see it in their faces as I'm speaking each weekend. They want to have a genuine, honoring relationship with the Lord. But here's the crucial point again: it's not just something you feel. Authentic faith actually involves something that you do. That's why we are continuing to explore God's Word for His instructions on developing the disciplines of a sincere faith—because there are actions you can actually take that lead to authenticity. We've been talking about them: prayer and Bible study. If you're having trouble tooling those things up, get some fasting going. I've re-engaged the discipline of fasting. And I can't believe the impact. All of a sudden, I just want to pray all the time now. I want to pray with everyone about everything. That's deepening my fellowship with others. This process is tuning up authenticity in my life. And I pray the same thing for you.

The focus of this chapter is the discipline of serving Jesus Christ. We're going to go to two passages of Scripture, both in the Gospels. These are from the lips of Jesus Christ Himself, the Master Teacher, the greatest Servant who came, **"not to be served, but to serve,"** the Bible says, **"and to give his life as a ransom for many."**[1]

Let's begin with Luke 17:7–10:

> **Will any one of you who has a servant plowing or keeping sheep say to him when he has come in from the field, "Come at once and recline at table"? Will he not rather say to him, "Prepare supper for me, and dress properly, and serve me while I eat and drink, and afterward you will eat and drink"? Does he thank the servant because he did what was commanded?**
> **So you also, when you have done all that you were commanded, say, "We are unworthy servants; we have only done what was our duty."**

Now let's talk about this matter of serving for a moment. And let me draw out a couple of thoughts I think you can see in this text. Here's the first one:

WE MUST NOT EXPECT GOD TO SERVE *US*
BEFORE WE HAVE SERVED HIM

The context here is very clear. Jesus is giving an illustration. He says, "You know, just imagine some guy who owns a farm. And it doesn't matter whether he's a sheep farmer or a crop farmer." The point is the servant (actually, the word there is *doulon*, or *slave*) was out working for his boss, serving him and doing his job. Servanthood was his identity, who he was—to carry out what the master wanted done.

So the servant comes in from a hard day's work. How do you generally feel at the end of a long day? You feel tired and hungry. Jesus pictures the slave walking in and maybe what he smells cooking stirs up even more hunger. But he's still a servant. So rather than focusing on what he needs and wants, he has to continually keep as his first priority the master—always the master first; never me first—always what God is doing first; not me—not what I want but what God wants. And even when I want the same thing God wants, I must pay attention to *when* He wants it. He is the Master; I am the servant. Jesus drives home the point: we must not expect God to serve us before we have served Him.

So let me ask you: Are you expecting some things from God? Have you been thinking, "Do you know what, God? I've done a lot! I have followed You. I have served You. And now I am expecting some things. I need this, God. And I don't mean by Friday—I need this now!" Sound familiar? Because here's the thing: the Lord really *does* a lot for us and the Lord *has done* a lot for us. But if *the only thing* God ever did for you was just keep you from hell, how could you not sing His praises through all eternity? Yet the Lord actually does far more for us than simply save us from hell. So our response to all this has to be our mindset. We can't say the Lord *doesn't* do for us, and we know we're invited to *ask* the Lord to do things for us. But if you forget you are a servant, and start thinking that God is the servant—that's a problem. You can think, "Well, I did my part, God. Now it's Your turn. I'm home, tired, and hungry. Feed me, God. Do what I want You to do and take care of these things." That response is not good. We are the servants; He's the Master. We've been bought with a price—He *owns* us.

In what ways are you expecting from God? Here are some ways we presume from God in matters He has *not* promised to follow our expectations:

#1 Protection for our children. I don't want my kids to get hurt. I don't desire for my family to be in any accidents, or have anything awful happen to them. I don't want my children or now my grandchildren to get off track and struggle spiritually. I'd rather they never have to go through a valley. "I want You to take care of them, God. Do You see me over here leading my small group, parking cars, working in the kitchen? I don't mind serving You, God, but I have some expectations." Really!? You're going to demand some kind of payback from God? Get ready for disappointment.

#2 Provision of financial wants. "I'm not willing to downsize, God. I've got a better plan—upsize every year. I'm not willing to cut back. I need the job that pays as much if not more as the last. I'm not going backwards in any way, God. That's what I expect from You." Those might be our thoughts; they are not what a servant thinks.

#3 Health and healing. Now the Lord *does* heal! But watch out when specific health or healing becomes an expectation. "I must have this, God. If You don't do this for me, I'm going to have some very harsh thoughts about You. If You don't fix this; if You don't sort this out; if You don't get me the test result I need . . ." Some of us have been through those valleys. And it's right to pray and ask God, but it's wrong to demand from God as though He owed it to us because of how we've served.

#4 Guidance. Given the way life is, it's likely you are facing a difficult decision right now. And there's an uncertain future including some hard choices to be made. You've been asking God for wisdom and you're tired of the way forward being cloudy and uncertain. You want to know! "I want certainty, God! I expect You to make this clear to me."

But we can't demand.

And then...

#5 Salvation of someone very dear to you, maybe a child or a parent or a sister or a lifelong friend. "C'mon, God. I'm serving You over here. Can't we get this person into heaven for me? Can't I apply some of my efforts for You as a kind of down payment on their behalf?"

But all these assumptions reveal we are overlooking one crucial fact. God is not a coin-operated deity. He is not automatic or mechanical. So when our child does get hurt, or we lose a job, or get a bad health report, our immediate response to God will show us a lot about expectations we might not have even realized we had. Watch out for any sort of equation-thinking where I do X, therefore God owes me Y.

We must not expect God to serve us *before* we have served Him or even *because* we have served Him. We're not in a position nor do we have nearly enough of the big picture to negotiate with God. We must trust Him and serve Him. We have His permission to ask but not to demand. Presenting our requests to the Lord always means leaving the final decision up to Him.[2]

WE MUST NOT EXPECT ANY IMMEDIATE *RETURN* FOR OUR SERVICE

We're back in Jesus' story in Luke 17. So this guy finishes work one day and comes in from the field. He announces: "All right—I'm back. Where is my dinner? Who cooked for me? I've worked and now I want someone to work for me." No, immediate gratification is not reality for a servant.

"Will any one of you who has a servant plowing or keeping sheep say to him when he has come in from the field, 'Come at once and recline at table'? Will he not rather say to him, 'Prepare supper for me, and dress properly, and serve me while I eat and drink, and afterward...'?" (vv. 7–8). It's not wrong to eat. It's not wrong to relax. But first things come first.

So we must not expect an immediate return for our service. Don't give with the motive of getting something back or you're going to be disappointed. Now the truth of this principle is illustrated in any situation where people are serving in some way in the church. Conversations with faithful servants are delightful; conversations with the other kind, not so much. When "conditional" servants are called for duty, the script often goes like this: "I know I said I would fill that role, but now I can't. And so I won't."

The caller asks, "Well, what's the problem?" If you have enough of those conversations with people, you find out their change of commitment occurred because they had certain expectations that were not met:

I didn't feel appreciated. Sometimes they'll say, "Well, I didn't feel valued. Nobody thanked me. No one wrote me a note. Not a single person said, 'I really appreciate what you do.'" Well, I hope Harvest is an appreciative church and I trust the same for your church. If I had a chance to talk to you and I knew what you were doing to serve the body of Christ, I would certainly thank you. And I hope others are grateful, too. But Matthew 25 and 1 Corinthians 3 make it really clear we serve the Lord Christ, and on *that day* we're going to get from Him a "thank-you" we can't imagine. But that day hasn't come yet! It's like you've been only been working for a week and payday is twice a month and you're upset you haven't gotten a paycheck yet. The payoff—the appreciation—comes from Jesus Christ Himself. We are serving Him.

So if your kids haven't risen up and called you blessed yet, and if nobody's figured out the kind of sacrifice you've been putting into the job, well, it's not over yet. Don't be impatient. And don't quit serving just because you don't feel appreciated.

Another reason why people do drop out of service is because they say . . .

I didn't get the results I wanted out of it. "I've poured myself into parenting." "I've given myself to this work." "I've exhausted myself in this service, and I thought I was . . ." Again, 1 Corinthians 3 says one planted and one watered, **". . . but God gave the growth"** (v. 6). You cannot control outcomes; all you can do is control effort. God is the One who produces the growth. I realize many churches work as hard as we do and serve as hard as we do and aren't seeing the fruit we see. And maybe you haven't seen the fruit yet. But you cannot demand that.

Some people say . . .

I didn't get the feeling I wanted. "I wanted to feel happy. I wanted to feel fulfilled." Hey—this will help. Ministry is hard work. Someone said, "You don't really know what it's like to be a servant until someone treats you like one." The word *toil* comes to mind. I'm not saying there's no joy in it, but it's intermittent joy. Unscheduled. Unexpected. There are seasons of exciting ministry, but the progression isn't under our control. The Master knows what He's doing.

Do you want to know how it goes? God's Word and generations of our predecessors give us a pretty good picture of the way God works. Each of the feelings or responses we just looked at are evidence that pruning has been going on. We base our decision to quit or retreat on these experiences, but God allows us to go through them because He is carrying out a plan. Here's the sequence:

You bear fruit.

Then you get pruned.

Then you bear more fruit.

If you don't quit, you get pruned again.

Kathy and I feel like our church—and certainly we as a couple—are in a season of more fruitfulness right now. Many of the members of our church have walked through a season of pruning with us. If we move through this season of more fruitfulness, guess what's coming? More pruning. I don't like getting trimmed. I don't like *watching* pruning and I don't like *being* pruned. But when the Lord has to come and say, "Look! This isn't helping. That is holding you back. What I'm about to do will make you stronger," we have to submit to God's work as the Master Gardener. This is the life of the follower of Jesus: seasons of fruitfulness followed by seasons of pruning, followed by seasons of greater fruitfulness. And if you veer off the track; if you end upside down in a ditch; if you quit serving because you can't get through a season of pruning, then you're going to miss a lot of the discipline that leads to authenticity.

And then here's the third lesson about serving:

WE MUST SEE OUR SERVICE AS OUR *OBLIGATION* TO JESUS CHRIST

Here again, Jesus' story in Luke 17 helps us see the point: **"So you also, when you have done all that you were commanded, say 'We are unworthy servants: We have only done what was our duty'"** (v. 10). *Duty* as used in this verse means *obligation*, what can reasonably be expected. Jesus is saying in effect, when you serve, all you are doing is your basic duty.

Our church did something wonderful for me and for my wife when I had my fiftieth birthday. One Saturday night, the congregation helped me celebrate the milestone. They brought in a number of people from Canada and from other places where we've served. They said some very kind words about our ministry. Our kids participated. I was blown away by the whole thing. I said to Kathy, "I don't think we've ever felt so loved in this church." The church is growing in love, and we experienced it firsthand. It was a huge deal.

But honestly, it was also a little uncomfortable. Sometimes it's just easier to serve than to let people serve you. And I kept thinking the whole time what an amazing blessing this was. So then they brought me up front and wanted me to talk. I didn't even *know* what to say. So I read Jesus' words, **"So you also, when you have done all that you were commanded, say 'We are unworthy servants. We have only done what was our duty'"** (v. 10).

By almost any measure, some people do a lot for the Lord. But don't ever let yourself develop the idea you're some elite Christian because you serve. You're just doing your job. Don't let yourself develop the expectation, "People need to acknowledge me. Others need to appreciate me. I do a lot." You are simply stepping up to your duty!

Now I'm going to make this just as focused as I can make it. I'm going to pick one person for a case study—you, the reader. First, I hope that you are a follower of Christ. Here's what's coming: you are under orders. And if I could just be a messenger on behalf of our Savior, Jesus Christ, let me remind you, He *commands* you to serve. Don't pray about it. Don't be like, "Well, sometimes we serve in the summer when our schedule is freed up." What?! This is your 24/7/365 card-carrying-follower-of-Jesus-Christ-member-of-the-family-of-God duty. Duty! Don't close this book and think,

> WE CAN'T GO WRONG IF WE SERVE LIKE JESUS, IF WE HAVE THE SAME ATTITUDE HE HAD.

"Pastor James said we should serve. Let's consider that possibility. Let's discuss the merits of serving Jesus." Don't talk or even pray about it! Just do it. Find a job among God's people. Roll up your sleeves. Do it—forever!

I can hear people raising their hands and asking, "When do I get a review?"

Not soon! Just do your job!

Others are thinking, "Man, you're making me feel uncomfortable. I don't think I'm going to come to any church that expects me to take my responsibility before Christ seriously!" Lame! That's an unacceptable excuse for shirking duty! We are making disciples here. If you want to sit in a church that will let you get a check mark for church attendance, it won't be here—off you go. It's our loss. We are sorry to lose you.

I don't want to build any more buildings with more seats for more people. I'm just looking for a roomful of disciples. A gathering of authentic believers can take over the world for Christ—if we follow Jesus and do our job.

When it comes to service, we don't really have to guess what that looks like. We've got the best example—Jesus Himself. He has never asked us to do something He didn't do Himself. We can't go wrong if we serve like Jesus, if we have the same attitude He had.

Let's go over to the gospel of John, and trace part of the last day of

Christ's ministry—John 13–17. We are in the final twenty-four hours before the cross. I want to point to some guidelines for us from Jesus' serving—one main point with some thoughts under it.

WE MUST SERVE *FAITHFULLY*

Now I didn't sit in my office and try to think up, "Well, what would be the best descriptor of service?" The concept of faithfulness is mentioned eighty-two times in the Scriptures, mainly by Jesus and Paul. Compared to patience as a quality, faithfulness is mentioned almost three times more frequently. Patience is important; faithfulness is crucial. We are told that when we stand before Jesus Christ someday, if we get the good report, we're not going to get, "You are *awesome!*" You are not going to get, "Wow! You rocked the world." Nobody's getting extra credit. The best Billy Graham can hope for is, **"Well done, good and faithful servant."**[3] That's the summa cum laude of feedback from Jesus Christ. It's the one quality we are all aspiring to: faithfulness.

Here's a definition of faithfulness: *constant in the performance of duty.* "I don't give up." "I don't shut down." "I just keep on doing the thing God has called me to do." I want to be faithful.

First Corinthians 4:2 is the New Testament classic passage that confirms faithfulness as the required characteristic of all stewards (one term for our role as believers): **"Moreover, it is required of stewards that they be found faithful."** When Paul instructs Timothy about the kind of men who will ensure the faith will be transmitted from one generation to another, he has one quality in mind: faithfulness. **"... and what you have heard from me in the presence of many witnesses entrust to faithful men who will be able to teach others also."**[4]

This will help. Let's follow Jesus' example through this extended passage in John 13.

We must serve faithfully ...

Even when my schedule is full.

"Now before the Feast of the Passover ..." (v. 1). Passover in

Jerusalem was the high point of every Jewish calendar. It was like New Year's Eve in Times Square—for days. The occasion remembered Israel's deliverance from Egypt under Moses. It was family time, spiritual time, and a party time! Jews from all over the world made the pilgrimage to David's city. Every child of Jacob hoped at least one time in his life to celebrate Passover in Jerusalem. Since the triumphal entry several days before, Jesus' life had been dawn-to-dark skirmishes with His enemies. The public tensions were high, and yet Jesus deliberately took time to be with His disciples.

John continues, **"when Jesus knew that his hour had come to depart out of this world to the Father"** (v. 1). Several times in the Gospels, Jesus referred to the fact that, **"My hour has not yet come."**[5] And now it says, **"Jesus knew that his hour had come."** Game on! The reason why He is here! He is about to go to the cross and suffer as an atoning sacrifice for sin! It's Passover. His hour had come.

Now many of us would have given Jesus a hall pass to say, at this point, "You know, I'd try to take care of you all, but I've got to get on My own program now. I've got to get focused on what's going to happen to Me in the next few hours. I'll be in touch." Now that would make sense, right? I mean, He is at prime time of why He came. I'm taking from Jesus' example that I also have to serve faithfully even when my schedule is full, even when I am the busiest, and even when I have the greatest demands upon me. Busy at the brink of a major trial, surely Jesus can think about Himself now. But He didn't excuse Himself, and we can't either.

Jesus shows us we can't answer the call like this: "Sorry, Pastor James. We can't serve right now. Our plate's loaded. We're going through a big trial." Or, "Sorry, Pastor Jeff. You can't count on us at the moment. We have a full schedule." Or even, "Remember our promise to participate, Pastor Mo? Well it's not going to happen. We're a little overcommitted." Really!?

We need to keep this picture in our minds. Jesus is about to go to the cross. He will soon perform the greatest act of service that has ever been performed. Yet He stays in the moment, serving. We must serve faithfully even when our schedule is full.

This past week I was blown away by a woman I talked to on the phone who is going through a trial. Her situation definitely stands out among the trials in our church right now! And trust me, some people in our church are going through some deep waters, deeper than most of us.

Yet in the midst of this deep, dark trial, with no end in sight, she and her husband started a ministry to help people going through what they're going through. She's turning a trial into gold and it isn't anywhere near over yet! Wow! I am so inspired and challenged by their faithful example. I am provoked to greater faithfulness myself.

Second, I must serve . . .

Even when I want to quit.

Notice the description continues in John 13:1, **". . . having loved his own who were in the world, he loved them to the end."** This doesn't mean Jesus was acting like nothing else was going on. The Bible also says that during these hours, as the cross drew near, **". . . Jesus was troubled in his spirit."**[6] As a man, He expected the betrayal, the pain, and the cross. As God, He anticipated the judgment of the Father.

As I said, no one would have criticized if He had said, "You know guys? This isn't a good time for Me. I hope you won't be offended, but I would rather be alone. I've taught you. I've tried to live it in front of you. I've pictured it a thousand times in a hundred different ways. I'm sorry, guys. But I have to get focused on My own thing, because it's going to take everything I've got." But notice, He **"loved them to the end."** Underline that in your Bible. That's a little great truth you can come back to: He loved them to the end. The word *them* includes you, and the phrase gives you a standard to live by.

Now church isn't always about the whole message. Sometimes church is about a word from God. This chapter may have the same effect. For you, Jesus' example above is the word God has for your life today. You are going to love someone to the end. You may be wondering, "How long is this going to go on?"

Be ready for the possible answer: "To the end—that's how long."

"How long am I going to stick with them?"

"To the end—that's how long you're going to stick with them."

"How long am I going to keep doing this, God? I think it's getting hard. I think it's time for me to start thinking about myself." Incorrect. It is not time to quit. You are a follower of Jesus Christ. He kept going; He will help you do the same.

You say, "I just don't think I can go on, James." No, you cannot. But in your desperation, you can find a provision of strength, wisdom, and endurance from the Lord you never thought possible. And it's right there for you. Go get it and recommit yourself. You are going to love, until when? To the end.

Even when my schedule is full. Even when I want to quit. This next one is also hard. Look at John 13:2.

Even when my heart is breaking.

"During supper, when the devil had already put it into the heart of Judas Iscariot, Simon's son, to betray him . . ." What?! One of the people He has loved to the end is going to betray Him. It must have been weird sitting at a table with a guy who sold you out, who said, "I know you are going to kill Him and I will give Him to you if you give me X."

"Fine, we'll give it to you."

"Thank you very much. I'll let you know the time and place you can pick Him up."

Now Jesus and Judas are sitting at the table. I grew up listening to Mom, with a flannel graph, telling vivid Bible stories. I always knew that Jesus and Judas were sort of enemies anyway. But that's the way a kid looks at it. That's not the way it really was. Jesus *loved* Judas. This had to be what was on His mind, because He deliberately included Judas in what He was about to do for all the disciples.

Psalm 41:9 describes this Judas prophetically: **"Even my close friend in whom I trusted, who ate my bread, has lifted his heel against me."**

So Jesus considered Judas a close friend. We know what was on Jesus' mind during the supper.

When you put all the accounts of the Last Supper in the Gospels together, a certain picture emerges from Jesus' statements:

"One of you will betray me."[7]

"He who has dipped his hand in the dish with me will betray me."[8]

"Behold, the hand of him who betrays is with me on the table."[9]

"Woe to that man by whom the Son of Man is betrayed!"[10]

"One of you will betray me."[11]

"It would have been better for that man if he had not been born."[12]

Six times in one meal, Jesus brings up His betrayer. Why? Because when your heart has been broken by the betrayal of another person, you can hardly finish a sentence without thinking of them. You can hardly go through a paragraph without having them come to mind. You could be standing in the shower or driving on the freeway or coming and going from the grocery store. And out of nowhere that person's face is in front of you, and what they've done is on your mind again. Jesus was crushed in His humanity by the action of His own friend! Surely He doesn't have to serve now!?

Yes, He showed us we must serve faithfully in the face of heartache.

So picture this now. A three-year ministry of the disciples is coming to an end. All the crowds are gone; the feeding of the 5,000; the healing—it is all done. Now it's just like final locker room talk and He is going to the cross.

Any suggestions about what Jesus should do?

How about a great sermon to bring them to their feet?

How about a mighty miracle to stretch their faith and shame their unbelief?

How about a bottom-line chalk talk on strategies for building the church so everything in Acts will go really well?

What's it going to be, Jesus?

Check this:

Jesus, knowing that the Father had given all things into his hands, and that he had come from God and was going back to God, rose from supper. He laid aside his outer garments, and taking a towel, tied it around his waist. Then he poured water into a basin and began to wash the disciples' feet and to wipe them with the towel that was wrapped around him.[13]

Sometimes you need to really look into what's there. Notice what He said. What did He say in this moment? He said *nothing*.

Even when we serve in silence.

Sometimes the time for talking is done. There are no more words to be said. Words can't fix this. We just need to serve. Do what is our duty to do. Just do it.

John painted such a picture here of humble, quiet service. Jesus doesn't announce Himself. He doesn't get up with some kind of, "Hey, boys? It goes like this!" Or, "Here's the part you're not getting," or, "Observe this world-class object lesson, boys." No lead line. No pointing it out.

It's important that we all understand—with all due respect to Leonardo da Vinci's Renaissance painting of the Last Supper—this was not thirteen guests in high-back thrones. Here were guys reclining on their sides with a block of wood in front of them and piece of bread on the wood and maybe something to drink. This was an upper room, with a rough wooden floor and perhaps thin mats for "seating." The men may have kicked off their sandals at the door, but their feet would have been caked with whatever they walked in during their trip from Bethany into Jerusalem. It would have been customary for a servant, a hired person—not the host; not the other quests—to take off their sandals and wash their feet in preparation for the meal. You don't have to be a genius to do the math on what had been overlooked. The two disciples who Jesus had sent to prepare the meal had forgotten a detail.[14] Without saying a word, Jesus silently transformed that oversight into a teachable moment for the ages.

We must serve quietly. And with three other qualities Jesus demonstrated simultaneously.

Serve Humbly, Mutually, Immediately. (John 13:6–17)

We actually know from the context recorded in Luke 22:24–30 what the disciples were doing when Jesus got up to wash their feet. They were arguing about who was the greatest! They were trash-talking when Jesus made His move.

One disciple said, "Why are we arguing? There's no question; I am the greatest!"

And another answered, "What are you talking about, man? *I'm* the greatest!"

"No, you say that all the time."

"Yeah, because it's true! That's why I say it."

And so the Twelve were trading jabs and put-downs. Then Jesus gets up. He doesn't say, "Knock it off!" Or even, "What's wrong with you guys?"

Now I want you to notice how the action words in these verses describe what Jesus did:

Rose.

Laid.

Took.

Tied.

Poured.

Washed.

Wiped.

John 13:4–5 describes how He went to work without a word, quietly, humbly. Repeating the actions with each disciple until He got to Peter. The big fisherman pulls his feet away: **"Lord, do you wash my feet?"** (v. 6). Peter misunderstands—it's just not right for Jesus to wash his feet. You know Peter, always the enthusiast. **"You shall never wash my feet"** (v. 8).

Now Peter is going too far, so Jesus gently brings him back: **"If I do not wash you, you have no share with me"** (v. 8).

In classic Peter style, he now goes overboard the other way, **"Lord, not my feet only but also my hands and my head!"** (v. 9). You're right, Lord, I don't get it, but I don't want to miss out on anything—give me the whole bath!

"Jesus said to him, 'The one who has bathed does not need to wash, except for his feet, but is completely clean. And you are clean, but not every one of you'" (v. 10). He mentioned the betrayal again. The big picture was on Jesus' mind as He continued to serve.

John 13:12 describes what happened next: **"When he had washed their feet and put on his outer garments and resumed his place, he said to them, 'Do you understand what I have done to you?'"** It's almost a question of desperation. It feels like He's implying, "Guys, time is running out here, and you were just arguing about who is the greatest. But this is it; do you understand what I have done for you? I am gone after this. Have you been listening to anything I've been saying?"

Jesus didn't wait for their response. He wanted them to feel the weight of what He had just done: **"You call me Teacher and Lord, and you are right, for so I am. If I then, your Lord and Teacher, have washed your feet, you also ought to wash one another's feet."** (vv. 13–14). I'm sure at first they were expecting Him to say, "you also ought to wash My feet!"

They were ready to respond, "Well, sure. We ought to wash Your feet. No problem." Then they would have started fighting over who got to wash Jesus' feet.

But Jesus surprised them again. "This is not a trade in services. I've set a standard I expect you to follow." Then He repeated Himself for emphasis: **"For I have given you an example, that you also should do just as I have done to you. Truly, truly, I say to you, a servant is not greater than his master, nor is a messenger greater than the one who sent him. If you know these things, blessed are you if you do them"** (vv. 15–17). Jesus didn't leave us without a clear example of what He expects from His servants. Whatever else is before us, we must *serve*.

Let me end this by telling you about Howard. He and his wife have been coming to Harvest for almost twenty years. Most of the people in our church don't even know him, and those who do, just know him as Howard. He's one of the ever-present guys who make the nuts, bolts, doorways, and bathrooms of a building designed for thousands of people to keep functioning the way they should. I see him outside in the parking lot of our church, helping people in the summer when it's boiling hot and in the winter when it's bone-chilling cold. He is such a faithful servant of Jesus Christ, doing for others because of what Christ has done for him. We've got a lot of Howards around our church. If your church functions as a caring body, you've got some Howards among your people, too. I'd like to encourage the Howards who might be reading this to keep up the good servant work. Let me urge you to keep doing even if no one recognizes you or thanks you. You've just got to keep doing the thing that God has called you to do because you're not even really serving the people in a church. You are serving the Lord. And is it hard sometimes? Do you want to quit sometimes?

Authentic faith pushes through the hardship and the temptation to quit. The most effective way to push is to serve. It's not that you don't recognize discouragement or feel disappointments; real service means you take one step after another because you're keeping your eye on **"Jesus, the founder and perfecter of our faith."**[15] The discipline of serving isn't hard to figure out. Jesus showed us how to do it. The discipline part comes when we decide to do what we know. Because, as Jesus succinctly put it, **"If you know these things, blessed are you if you do them."**[16]

THE REAL THING:

Discovering Spirit-Worship

THE FIRST TIME I EVER EXPERIENCED what I would call spirit-worship, our spirit with God's Spirit, was in the early '80s. I've explained and retold these events in several places, but they continue to be the root God has used to nourish much of my thinking about the kind of worship that provokes God's glory to be seen. I had to discover firsthand the immense difference between worshiping God from your head and worshiping God with your spirit. I had to learn the discipline of worship.

On a trip out west, I visited the original Calvary Chapel in Costa Mesa in Los Angeles. One of the lasting but subconscious impressions I had when I arrived was a sense of purpose for the gathering. There was expectation in the air. I might have guessed at the time that these people were just excited about being together; now I realize I was among people who were actually anticipating meeting with God!

In the first forty-five minutes of the worship service, I felt myself powerfully drawn in to an atmosphere where people were singing—I had never heard this before—*singing to God*. They were singing from their spirits to God. They were creating new music that echoed Bible themes and directed them back to God. These were love songs to the Lord. The impact on me was physical, emotional, and awesome. I wept as I realized I was in God's presence.

Not only was the direction of the singing new to me, I had *never* been in a setting where the glory of God was so manifest among His people. It was so intimate, genuine, personal, and as I now think of it—vertical. In our praise and worship, God had come down to be among us! Even the act of remembering those moments still overwhelms me with a sense of wonder and gratitude for God's gift to me that night.

Even songs or hymns I was familiar with took on a different tone and texture when I realized they had been written by our forefathers to be sung to God, and we had just gotten used to singing them to each other. For example, a majestic hymn like *Great Is Thy Faithfulness* is a classic of true worship that can be lifted by spirit-filled worshipers. And yet the familiarity of the lyric, the archaic "Thy," and the failure to acknowledge we are approaching the Holy of Holies with these words on our lips make the singing, even accompanied by orchestra and scored with great harmony, fall short of spirit-worship. We are left moved by the sheer beauty of the music, but with an unfulfilled longing because our voices haven't expressed our spirits' hunger to acknowledge God in His presence.

That evening I couldn't deny that I sensed God's Spirit there, responding and delighting in the praises of His people. The experience just rocked me. It was like nothing I'd ever seen before. I had participated in lots of singing about God, but singing *to* God was an exciting new frontier I never wanted to leave. I was ready to make it my home. Since then, I have practiced and taught that the way we plan and prepare for worship must be a thoughtful, enthusiastic, whole-person encounter with God that includes spirit expression. God meets us vertically! We know we are on the mark when we can describe the experience as an earth-shattering, window-rattling, life-altering encounter with God. There's power in spirit-filled worship. This is why, as you will see in this chapter, the discipline of worship energizes all the other disciplines. Increased worship is the reason we undertake the disciplines in the first place, and if the outcome of our efforts isn't a heightened and humbling sense of God's presence and the life-sustaining need to experience *That* presence, then the disciplines have not accomplished their purpose.

CHAPTER SEVEN

THE DISCIPLINE OF WORSHIP

What is authentic worship? Throughout this book we have been using the term *discipline* to describe practices and principles that we can put into action in growing a sincere faith. We ended the last chapter with the words of Jesus ringing in our souls: **"If you know these things, blessed are you if you do them."**[1] This book has been not only about *knowing* what to do when it comes to a living faith but also about what it takes to *do these things*. Worship is at the center of everything we do that leads to blessing. In fact, worship is the reason you and I exist. So, anything we can do to sharpen our discipline of worship will lead to blessing.

God energizes worship. I can't explain it to you exactly, but when the God of the universe is rightly worshiped, powerful things happen. When God's people gather, God Himself longs to join in more so when we're together than even when we're apart. And when God is rightly worshiped, truly awesome things happen in the lives of people. God things start occurring. And He blesses the gathering and those who participate. Now, in order to verify these claims we need to talk about what it means, really, to worship God. How do we practice the discipline of worship? Are you sure you know these things? And are you doing them?

THE PATTERN OF WORSHIP

The passage that will serve as the foundation for this chapter is the most extensive teaching that Jesus Christ does on this subject of worship. Let's return to John 4 to study this concept: the pattern of worship. The first thing we need to get on the table is a definition itself. Even before we read the Scriptures, do we understand what we mean by the word *worship*? You may have all sorts of ideas come into your head when you hear the term. There are actually many words in Scripture translated worship: *praise* or *adore*, *magnify*, *rejoice*, *give thanks*—all of these and more are components or aspects of worship. Literally on every page of the Bible is this idea of worshiping God. We are created and saved to the praise of His glory. We were made to worship.

Now some people ask, "Well, who is this God exactly? And what kind of a God needs and wants to be worshiped? It sounds as though He might be very proud—even arrogant and self-absorbed. Or maybe all this desire for praise reveals God as insecure. Why would He need affirmation from us if He's God?"

Now, I don't want to hurt your feelings, but those are kindergarten thoughts about God. It's time to grow up into Him. What you're confusing is this: God is not a human being. He doesn't function like a human being. We don't understand Him by extending human behavior and attaching it to Him. We think it's arrogant for one human being to want the adulation of other human beings, because we all recognize that human beings, for the most part, are not qualitatively different one from another. We understand that one person is not that much better than another person. But God is not some exalted human being at the top of the mankind pyramid. God is a being in an entirely different category, where He is the only member. God is ineffable glory. He dwells in unapproachable light. He is not like us at all. He says, **"For as the heavens are higher than the earth, so are my ways and my thoughts than your thoughts."**[2] The amazing thing is not that God invites our worship; the amazing thing is that He accepts from us what He does not need. The more you study this, the more you begin to understand God is leading us to the place of worship because in His presence is the place we rightly belong. Whether we realize it or not, we need to worship. We were designed in such a way that worship is good for us!

The word *worship* in the Old Testament means, literally, *to bow before.* It's the idea of actually pressing your forehead right to the ground. The term expresses extreme humility and recognition of the infinite superiority of the one who is worshiped. In the New Testament there are two words in Greek: one of them (*proskuneo*) means *to kiss toward*, or *to kiss the hand*, conveying the idea of adoration; the other word (*latreuo*) means *to give or to pay homage*. It also means *to ascribe worth or value*. So much of what passes for worship in the church today is really just the exaltation of self. If you listen to current worship music, a lot of it is singing about self and what God does for me and how He benefits me. Those sentiments are a long way from true worship. Authentic worship ascribes worth to God. The essence of worship can be found in the first of the Ten Commandments: **"You shall have no other gods before me."**[3] That actually means "no other gods before, after, or alongside Me"—there's only room for one true God, Maker of heaven and earth. Anything or anyone else going by the title *god* is a fake and impostor.

When I look at my life and recognize I have allowed anything to accumulate on the table of my heart and mind that occupies my time and attention in a worshipful way—that's a problem! Sweeping all of those things off so only God remains is my ultimate reality. I am for Him, breathing for Him, living for Him, and spending my life for Him. God in the center of my attention is the essence of worship. It's one of the reasons why we come to church: to sweep stuff off the table that has gotten into the place where only God belongs.

Most of us are aware of some of these distractions away from God, but here are the results of another of our helpful surveys. We've asked a hundred people and ranked the top five answers to this question: name something we worship instead of God:

Number five: We place our family on a pedestal for worship. We can let our children or our spouse get in the place of God. Our families are our primary responsibility God has given us; that's why they can never come before Him. If we make them more important than God in our lives, we have failed to do what God wants us to do for them!

Number four: material things, including money. We easily worship money instead of God. Jesus said, **"Do not lay up for yourselves treasures on earth . . . For where your treasure is, there your heart will be also."**[4] When we worship God, we treasure Him and recognize His worth—but if we set our hearts on our treasure, our money, it has displaced God and we're in trouble.

Number three: sports figures, people from Hollywood. We worship those people when we think "Oh, if only I could be like that person." That's worship. Do people even know the deeper significance of naming a television program *American Idol*? People are worshiping other people.

Number two: job, work, and career. People trust these fragile achievements will give their life meaning and significance, the very qualities only God can supply.

Number one: ourselves. We turn our needs and what we want into our highest pursuit. When we can't accept anyone, not even God, getting in the way of what we desire, we're worshiping the idol in the mirror.

The discipline of worship is a deliberate act where we sweep clean the table of our hearts and remove all the pretenders who would demand our worship. We gather with others in God's presence and ask Him to burn away all dross and worthless stuff that would crowd out God's rightful place. That's worship at its best—the kind of worship atmosphere where God shows up in glory.

You say, "Now I'm ready go back into John chapter 4." You will recall that we visited this passage back in the chapter on the discipline of fasting. Jesus was dealing with the Samaritan woman, known as the woman at the well. He asked her for a drink and then they got talking about the living water, which is Jesus Christ Himself. When we pick up the story at verse 16, Jesus has just turned a corner in the conversation. **"Jesus said to her, 'Go call your husband and come here.'**

The woman answered him, 'I have no husband.'

Jesus said to her, 'You are right in saying, "I have no husband"; for you have had five husbands, and the one you now have is not your husband'" (vv. 16–18). I mean, how brutal would it be to have a conversation with Jesus, right? He knows everything and He just cuts right to the heart of the matter. But wait a second; doesn't Jesus know us just as intimately today as He knew that woman at the well? And isn't it a phenomenal thing about the Lord to know we can drop all of our posing, posturing, and look-at-me, or aren't-I-a-good-boy, and be who we really are, who He already knows we are? Yet He loves us and even in our imperfection and sinfulness, He invites—He elicits our worship.

So Jesus' apparent straight talk was not hard with this woman but tender and truthful. He was direct in saying, "Hey girl, why don't you drop your guard a little bit. I *know* you, and I'm still talking to you!"

She was so stunned by His comment that all she could think to say was—talk about an understatement—**"Sir, I perceive that you are a prophet"** (v. 19). Ding. The clue bell just sounded. But in her first try she doesn't have the half of it yet. Plus, talking to a prophet might turn out to be a little dangerous. So she does the masterful thing we all do when we're under conviction; she changes the subject.

Her strategy was, "Hey, why don't we have a little seminar on worship here. You're a Jew; I'm a Samaritan. Let's compare notes."

Jesus' response? "Well, all roads lead back to Me. You want to talk about worship, let's talk worship."

She says in verse 20, **"Our fathers worshiped on this mountain, but you say that in Jerusalem is the place where people ought to worship."** She was a Samaritan. They only believed the first five books of the Bible. They picked the part they wanted, and then insisted that worship should be on Mount Gerizim (in their territory), not in Jerusalem.

Again, Jesus caught her by surprise: **"Woman, believe me, the hour is coming when neither on this mountain nor in Jerusalem will you worship the Father"** (v. 21). In other words, He's telling her, "Let Me give you some understanding. True worship is not about going out in your backyard, climbing up on the closest hill, and saying some random God-stuff. You can't just pick and choose what you want to do with God."

Worship Requires Understanding

Jesus now says this important phrase at the beginning of verse 22, **"You worship what you do not know."** Worship requires understanding. You can't just enter into some random worship relationship with God. Jesus is giving her a gentle rebuke: "Hey, you can't pick and choose the parts of the Bible you want. You can't craft God in your own image and say, 'Well, this is the God I want: all love, no justice; all convenience, no conviction.' If you try, you'll end up with something other than God."

I was talking to a man on a golf course recently. We had never met before. About an hour into our round of golf, I began to share the Lord with him. His response to my introducing Christ in the conversation was, "Oh spirituality; that's very important."

I said, "Tell me what you mean by that."

He said, "Well, I think people should have spiritual feelings and spirituality should be a part of your life."

"You mean like, random spiritual thoughts?" I asked.

He said, "Well, you know; whatever is meaningful to you."

Now, "whatever is meaningful to you" is not worship or even serious thinking about God. I went on to share with him some more, but the point is this: Jesus would have rightly said to that man, "You worship what you don't know." You must have some accurate information in order for your worship to be right. You can go off in the woods and make up god in your head if you want to. But that's what you'll have: a god you've made up. That god exists only as long as you let it. But there is a real God and He wrote a book and He has a Son. You can worship the true God if you will do the second thing Jesus told this woman.

Understanding Leads to Relationship

Back to John 4:22, where Jesus says, **"You worship what you do not know; we** [speaking of the Jewish people] **worship what we know, for salvation is from the Jews."** Think about that phrase: **"we worship what we know; for salvation is from the Jews."** Make a note of this: understanding leads to relationship. Personal knowledge is where the worship has to begin—with our relationship with Jesus Christ. When He said, **"... salvation is from the Jews,"** what did He mean? Well, read the Old Testament. All the promises were given to Abraham; the first five books of the Bible given to Moses; and Jesus Christ, the long-promised Messiah—all Jewish. All the greatest benefits that God has wanted to give this world have come through the funnel of the Jewish people. So Jesus could rightly say, **"salvation is from the Jews."**

But we also need to understand what the word *salvation* means. The word summarizes forgiveness of sins, rescue from the road to hell, and the gift of eternal life. **"God so loved the world, that he gave his only Son, that whoever believes in him should not perish but have eternal life."**[5] The gift of eternal life—have you received that by faith? Do you know Christ personally? Have you turned from your sin? Are you sure?

You say, "Well, I think I might have."

Don't roll the dice on this one, okay? This is a really big deal. If you think you *might* have, you haven't. You can only know or be confused. But

> THE DECISION TO TRUST CHRIST IS THE BEGINNING OF WORSHIP. THERE IS NO WORSHIP COMING APART FROM THAT DECISION.

you could move from confusion to knowing today. Jesus said, **"Whoever comes to me I will never cast out."**[6] And God promised that whoever would receive His Son would be given the authority to be called a child of God.[7] This could be your day to turn from your sin and embrace Christ by faith.

The decision to trust Christ is the beginning of worship. Please understand; there is no worship coming apart from that decision. That's why Jesus said to the woman, "Hey, you worship what you don't know and salvation is from the Jews, but I'm about to reveal to you that salvation." Worship has to begin with a relationship with God. That's the pattern of worship: understanding followed by relationship.

THE PRIORITY OF WORSHIP

The passage we are studying includes the most influential verses regarding the way we at Harvest practice the discipline of worship. Jesus said in John 4:23, **"But the hour is coming, and now is here, when the true worshipers will worship the Father in spirit and in truth."** In the gospel of John, the word *hour* refers to the cross. Almost every time Jesus makes statements like: "my hour is not yet come," "not until the hour," and "then at the hour"—it's all about the cross. The cross was continually on Jesus' mind. When He said, **"The hour is coming, and is now here,"** He was thinking of His death and all that it would set in motion. Amazing.

Ignorant Worship

Jesus moves from the "where" to the "who" of worship. He says, **"... when the true worshipers."** Now, if there are *true* worshipers, then there are also *false* ones. Some will practice worship; others will pretend to worship. Here's the question: Which are you? Are you a true worshiper or a false worshiper? Or, to put it another way, is your worship authentic? Before you answer, you may want to submit to Jesus' test. After all, He just pointed out to the woman she was an ignorant worshiper. He said, **"You worship what you do not know."** Like the woman at the well, we face the same choice between making a god up to suit our tastes or worshiping the one, true God who has revealed Himself in His Son, Jesus Christ. The choice is ours.

Hypocritical Worship

But ignorant worship is only one kind of false worship. Here's another kind: hypocritical worship. This kind of "worship" occurs when we show up for church to get an A for attendance, but our heart is far from God. You go through the motions, but you are thinking of things you've said and done this week you couldn't possibly reveal to the people around you. That's s hypocritical worship. Yours is the story of the prodigal son in Luke 15 before he realized what a mess he had made of his life. He was working with the pigs by day and in the evening remembering he still had a father at home, but was not yet ready to face the reality of going back. The formerly hypocritical son came home prepared to be the lowest slave in the household only to be welcomed as a son. Many of us can identify with that part of the story—but not all of us. Some of us are not the prodigal son; we're the older brother. We're the ones who always did the right thing, always said the expected things, and always sang the correct song. We carried our Bible—but our heart is far from God. That's also hypocrisy. We get an A for performance, an F for reality. Friends may be fooled by our appearances; God looks at our heart. You can't fool God or trick Him with hypocritical worship.

Apathetic Worship

Beyond ignorance or hypocrisy, true worship rejects apathetic participation. This is when time in church is so mindless and on automatic pilot that people can and often do sleep through the service. They remind me of the little boy standing outside a traditional church, looking at a war memorial plaque. When the pastor walked by and asked him what he was doing, the boy said, "I'm looking at the names of all the people who died in the service . . . but I do have a question."

The pastor said, "Yes, son, what's your question?"

"Well it doesn't say which service they died in—was it in the nine or the eleven o'clock service?" And yet too many people attend a church like that. The apathy is apparent in every pew and you can't wait to get out. Or maybe you bring the apathy with you. You can see that God is touching other people and moving in their lives, but you sit here and feel nothing. It's just dead to you; nothing's stirring in your heart. It's a massive effort to survive a service, or you just don't care. Apathy has no more part in true worship than ignorance or hypocrisy.

Jesus continued in John 4:23, **". . . for the Father is seeking such people to worship him."** That's the best news I've heard in a long time. God is looking for worshipers. God is seeking. I hear a lot of talk in the church today about seekers and people who are seeking God. I don't see very much of that in the Bible. I don't see people seeking God. In fact, Romans 3 says, **". . . no one seeks for God."**[8] People don't seek God; God seeks people. God forgive us for our man-centered understanding of how the relationship happens. God goes and finds people. Jesus said, **"The Son of Man came to seek and to save the lost."**[9] He told the parable of the shepherd who left the ninety-nine and went seeking after the one.[10] You say, "Well, I think I'm one of those ones." Did he find you?

Baptismal services here at Harvest are frequent and amazing. It's not unusual for hundreds to come to declare their faith in Christ in this way. And once you have listened in a single afternoon to a 140 people talk about the way God sought them and found them, you know how it happens. The stories are remarkably the same! It goes like this: "I was going along and I thought I was too sexy for my shirt; sure I had it all together and confident I knew what life was all about. Then all of a sudden, God dropped this *boulder* on my life and crushed me. He finally got my attention." It's always the same story. Now, the label on the boulder changes: a health crisis, a marriage breakdown, a collapse in a career, a bankruptcy, a personal, profound loneliness that wouldn't go away—the boulder titles vary, but it's always the same sequence. "I thought I was so cool and BAM! God found me." Then this little hand comes out from underneath the rock and a muffled voice says, "Maybe You could help me with my life. I thought I didn't need You and now I find out, I do. I really do." So that's how salvation happens—God finds us and gets our attention. And those people He finds *really* want to worship God.

Now, when you think about the ways God reached them, you might be tempted to ask them, "Don't you hate God for dropping that boulder on you?" No, here's the amazing thing: they don't. Once they figure out what happened, they say, "Man, without that big rock I would have never found God. I would have never loved God if God hadn't lovingly crushed me first."

If your response to what you just read is, "I've never been under any boulders"—well, your time's coming. Maybe your time has come. "Oh, I don't need God, I don't need all this"—we're waiting for the party when you figure out how wrong you are. You *do* need God.

"Oh, God is a crutch for some people." Ding! When you realize you are a spiritual cripple, that's just about the best day of your life. The Bible says that God is not willing that any should perish.[11]

A lady came up to me after a service, saying, "Oh, I'm so burdened for my husband; what if God doesn't do something?"

"Listen," I said, "God's doing a lot already." Every person's life has enough reasons to figure out they need God. The question is, will they humble themselves and respond to His seeking?

When you read a verse that tells you God is seeking worshipers,[12] don't you mentally raise your hand and think, "Pick me, Lord! Pick me?" Remember when you were a kid and they'd always choose up sides on the playground? I was always one of the last kids picked. I know what it's like to stand there the whole time, hoping to be the next one picked—but here's the good news: every single person can be chosen by God to be one of His worshipers. God is seeking such to worship Him. It's what God wants; worship is what we were created to do.

THE POWER OF WORSHIP

Now, let's talk about the power of worship. John 4:24 was on my lips before Harvest Bible Chapel ever began, and it has shaped our worship. **"God is spirit, and those who worship him must worship in spirit and truth."** In other words, because God is spirit, we must worship with our spirit.

There's a lot of theological debate about the nature of man. The Bible doesn't give us a clear anthropology—the specifics of human makeup. Some people say that man is body and soul. Those people are called *dichotomists* (dicha, two; temnein, cut). When they slice people, they only come up with two parts. Others would say that man is body, soul, and spirit. They are called *trichotomists*. People ask, "Well, James, what do you believe?" I believe that I don't know. And I'm starting a new movement where pastors admit when they don't know. The Bible doesn't settle the issue, so it doesn't make sense to claim to know more than we know. Here's what I can say confidently: sometimes it says "body-soul," sometimes it says "soul and spirit," sometimes it says, as we'll see later, "heart, soul, mind, and strength." Here's what I do know: every person in this universe created by God has a soul. The soul is made up of mind, emotions, and will. I believe when a person comes to Christ, God makes their soul alive.

Until then, every person outside of Christ, their soul is dead to God.[13] Every baby in our nursery on Sunday morning is dead as a doornail to God.

You say, "I don't believe that."

Believe it. We are born dead in our trespasses and sins, and it's only through repentance and faith that we are made alive by the Spirit of God; we become alive to God. And when we're made alive to God, we can begin to communicate to God with our spirits.

Now I'm going to go out on a limb and say something really bold right here: most people, even followers of Jesus Christ, do not know what it is to worship God with their spirit—spirit with Spirit, communicating with God. Most of us know how to worship with God the way we interact in a physics class—primarily a mental exercise. But spirit-worship involves the mind (thinking), will (acting and doing), *and* our spirit, especially our emotions, communicating with God, dropping our guard.

I grew up in a church that was all truth worship. But Jesus said, **"God is spirit!"**[14] It's an important point. We have to communicate with God from our spirit to His Spirit.

This is what I mean by truth-worship in the church of my youth. We'd sing great hymns and other songs that had so much majestic theology, but the truth came racing by at a thousand miles per hour and all you could say at the end of it was, "Wow, that's *really* true." It was an exchange of factual information about almighty God. We were learning and repeating what we learned—but our spirits were rarely engaged in worship.

What God wants to know is not, "Do you know this about Me?" but, "Do you care about the things that you know about Me?" Response is essential—your spirit responding and resonating with the truth your mind knows about God. When you start to get those things together, some powerful things happen.

Worship Brings God's Presence

You ask, "What is the power in worship?" Start with this: authentic worship brings God's presence. Psalm 22:3 says, **"Yet you are holy, enthroned on the praises of Israel."** That word *enthroned* is used a thousand times in the Old Testament and it means *the place where someone resides or dwells*—where they sit. The old translation (King James) said God *inhabited* the praises of His people. We could translate it: God sits down and settles into the praises of His people. He's comfortable there.

When you and I are standing up, that's a more formal position. When we sit we relax and settle in. But don't miss the whole picture: God is seated and His people are standing around Him. Now if you were to come into a large room, and everyone was standing except for the person in the center who was seated, you would think, "Whoa, that person is very important. Everyone is standing in their honor." That's the picture of God being enthroned in the praises of His people.

Something special happens when we get together and worship God in spirit and truth. God is enthroned. We want God to sit down and be comfortable and blessed as we praise, worship, and acknowledge who He is. I'm coming to *that* party. Worship brings God Himself.

I have the privilege of talking to a lot of people who come to our church for the first time as we pursue this thing called spirit-and-truth worship. Just recently I heard someone say, "I didn't know what I was missing." They were missing spirit *and* truth. Someone else said to me, "I hadn't met with God like that in a long time." Spirit and truth, coming together, this is where God manifests Himself to His people.

And not only does God show up with His presence, but when His presence comes, some really cool things follow.

Worship Brings Salvation

When God is rightly worshiped, lives are transformed by the cross of Jesus Christ. That's what we mean by worship brings salvation. Many people suggest today that you shouldn't have nonbelievers in a worship service. They say, "Well, they'll get freaked out; they don't want to sing; they won't want to participate—." Now, those horizontal analyses can be helpful in a way, but at the end of the day, I don't really care what *people* think about nonbelievers in worship services; I want to know what *God* says about it. First Corinthians 14 tells us what happens when a nonbeliever comes into an authentic worship service. Verse 23 says, **"If, therefore, the whole church comes together and all speak in tongues . . ."** That's speaking to God in some sort of a prayer language. Some people today, I believe, have that gift; others do not. But supposing you had a church where almost everybody had that gift, and they were speaking to God in those languages, what would happen if a nonbeliever came in? Paul says, **". . . and outsiders or unbelievers enter, will they not say that you are out of your minds?"** The possibility of confusion is why we don't encourage the public demonstration of those gifts in our services at Harvest. So, should nonbelievers not come to church? The next verse says, **"But if all prophesy . . ."**[15] (not everyone speaking in tongues or swinging from the chandeliers so they think we're nuts), he says, **"But if all prophesy."** What does he mean, *prophesy*? Second Peter 1:19 tells us, **"And we have the prophetic word more fully confirmed, to which you will do well to pay attention as to a lamp shining in a dark place."** Peter goes on to connect the mention of prophecy as a reference to God's Word: **"... knowing this first of all, that no prophecy of Scripture comes from someone's own interpretation. For no prophecy was ever produced by the will of man, but men spoke from God as they were carried along by the Holy Spirit"** (vv. 20–21). In our context today, everyone prophesying means everyone exhorting, singing, and speaking about what God's Word says.

Now just imagine a church where God's Word is so respected and elevated that in all of our conversations, in our preaching, and in our singing, the focus is on what God says, what God says, what God says. And imagine all of those multiple times when God is speaking, and we're attentive, echoing what God is saying—what happens if an unbeliever comes into *that* situation? Buckle your seat belt, here's what happens. First Corinthians 14:24 says, **"if all prophesy and an unbeliever or an out-sider enters, *he is convicted by all.*"** God's Word provokes *conviction*, that strong, sometimes overwhelming sense that what is being said applies *to you*. The lights suddenly go on and the view is shattering. For many believers, this is exactly what happened when God made His move. This may be *your* story. You came into a place where everyone was speaking God's Word and you were so convicted, you found yourself thinking, "I can't speak about God that way. I don't have that kind of relationship with Him. What do they have that I don't have?" Paul's not finished: **"he is convicted by all; he is called to account by all ..."** (v. 24). In the presence of Christ's Spirit, conviction is rapidly followed by accountability. "Why do they have something intimate with God and all I have is this generic spirituality, or nothing real at all, or just a lot of questions and no answers?"

I recently read from the memoirs of Malcolm X's third daughter. You are probably familiar with the story of Malcolm X, an African-American

Muslim leader killed in 1965. Malcolm X's wife, Betty, used to take their daughters to mosque every Sunday. But when they visited family in Philadelphia, they went to the Friendship Baptist Church where their grandparents attended. Malcolm X's third daughter, Ilyasah, says that she enjoyed especially the praying, testifying, and the singing of gospel music at that church. She said, "I loved the singing that went on, and I wanted to feel whatever powerful force was causing all these people to sing and clap so heartily." This is Malcolm X's daughter, drawn into an atmosphere where the true God was being worshiped. She goes on to wistfully say, "I never did catch the spirit, but I always kept the hope."[16] How sad that is; she was very close to the kingdom of God, yet has apparently never entered.

> THE VERY BEST COMMENT ANYONE COULD EVER GIVE ABOUT OUR CHURCH WOULD BE: *GOD IS THERE.*

First Corinthians 14 goes on to describe what can happen to that unbeliever under the full power of God's presence: **"the secrets of his heart are disclosed, and so, falling on his face, he will worship God and declare that God is really among you"** (v. 25). The very best comment anyone could ever give about our church would be: *God is there.* There is *nothing* better we can offer anyone than let them meet God. *Everything* else is secondary. Everything else is only significant to the degree that it helps people move from where they are and into God's presence. At Harvest, every weekend we have a team whose ministry is to bathe the services in prayer. Before, during, and after worship service, people are fervently asking for the manifest presence of God in response to worship.

We have stories about people who spotted our church in Rolling Meadows, Illinois, just off the freeway. They were desperate, and with nowhere else to turn, pulled into our parking lot and wandered into the worship center. There was nothing official going on, but the doors were open. They entered what we have come to know as the holy place where we meet God. And there might not have been any other people around, but these strangers were so moved by the Spirit of God in the place, they broke down and wept and turned their heart over to the Lord. Now, only God can do that and the power comes from the worshiping community. The people of God coming together and calling out to God, "Oh God, do for us what we cannot do for ourselves." God hears. And He answers.

Worship Brings Victory

Authentic worship creates an atmosphere where victory can be seen—God's victory. Worship puts everything else in perspective. Reading these chapters on spiritual disciplines may have left you feeling like your life is going around and around and not moving ahead spiritually like you want to. Rather than bringing hope of a way forward, these disciplines have catalogued your defeats. It's easy to think, "Well, when I get to a better place spiritually, and if I can just get a little victory in my life, then I'm going to come back to God in a big way." No, that plan will keep you in confusion and defeat. All first steps are *toward* God. Don't try to fix yourself and then come to God. Come to God, He'll fix it. God will do the repairs and restoration when you bring your confused, defeated, and frustrated self into His presence in surrender. It's never news to God that we're helpless! Genuine worship allows us to see more and more clearly how awesome God is and how very much we depend on Him. Worship brings salvation and victory.

Second Chronicles 20 describes the children of Israel obeying when God sent them out into battle with no bows and arrows, no spears, no shields—just trumpets, horns, and worship. They had been told, **"Thus says the LORD to you, 'Do not be afraid and do not be dismayed at this great horde, for the battle is not yours but God's'"** (v. 15). (How often does life look to you like a horde about to engulf you?) Instead of preparing for war, they engaged in worship. They prayed and then chose a worship band to lead them in praise. Instead of a battle cry, they lifted their voices in this great chorus: **"Give thanks to the LORD, for his steadfast love endures forever!"** (v. 21). We may think, "Who does something like that?" but the fact is, God's people stepped out in worship and the Scriptures record the powerful way God showed up: **"And when they began to sing and praise, the LORD set an ambush against the men of Ammon . . . so that they were routed"** (v. 22). See, there's something truly awesome that happens—God moves *toward* those who are worshiping Him.

God hasn't changed the way He responds to worship. **"Draw near to God, and he will draw near to you."**[17] Worship brings victory. If you are struggling with a temptation or frustration today, the first step is worship. Move more fully into the life of worship in the company of other believers. In God's presence, in the Holy of Holies, every spiritual discipline becomes doable. Prayer, Bible study, fasting, fellowship, and service become the outflow of worship, and they quickly lose their direction and power if they are not continually energized by worship. Worship always adds the *"who we're doing this for"* to what can otherwise become just the "what *we're doing"* of the spiritual disciplines. Authenticity in the life of a follower of Jesus can always be traced back to worship. It will always be the result of spending time in God's presence.

Worship Brings Healing

The last powerful thing we will mention is the discipline of worship brings healing. Jeremiah 17:14 says, **"Heal me, O LORD, and I shall healed; save me, and I shall be saved, for you are my praise."** We trust the Lord for healing day by day and we trust Him for our eternal salvation. What *we* do is praise! Malachi 4:2 declares, **"But for you who fear my name** (the fear of the Lord defines worship) **the sun of righteousness shall rise with healing in its wings."**

I don't believe in healers on demand. I don't believe that the apostolic gift of being able to say, "In the name of Jesus of Nazareth, rise up and walk," and immediate access to God's healing power is operating in the church today. I think there are some people who are pretending it does, but I don't see a lot of people walking up to blind people and saying, "In the name of Jesus, you can see." But I do believe that God heals people. I believe that God brings healing according to James chapter 5: **"Let** him call for the elders of the church, and let them pray over him" (v. 14). And there's *never* doubt about the source of healing: **"the Lord will raise him up"** (v. 15). We've seen people healed in our church, but always through coming first to the place of worship. Not, "Oh God, heal me! Preserve and protect all my idols collected around me." Instead, moving all of those distractions off the table and coming to a place where life is offered to God without demands, only trust. Those who have sickness in body hold their life out to God, learning to genuinely say, "Lord, give me life or take my life, do what pleases You, Lord." That kind of surrender to God is at the heart of worship. I've seen people come to that place and God healed them. And I've also seen people come to that place and God took them. But the place God is trying to get every person to is a deep recognition: "My life belongs to You, God. You are everything to me." That is the essence of worship. The closer you come to the Holy of Holies, the closer you have come to the place of ultimate healing.

THE PRACTICE OF WORSHIP

Because worship is a spiritual discipline, we must close with some practical applications on the practice of worship. In Mark 12, Jesus was asked, "What is the greatest commandment?" Jesus answered, **"The most important is, 'Hear, O Israel: The Lord our God, the Lord is one. And you shall love the Lord your God with all your heart and with all your soul and with all your mind and with all your strength'"** (vv. 29–30).

The summarized commandment means, love God, or worship God, with *all* that you are. But wait; the parts we use in loving God matter. Let's look at those parts for a moment.

Thoughtful worship

Since we're looking at *all* of *everything* that we are, we can begin with loving and worshiping God with our mind. "Love the Lord your God with all your mind." God wants us to think great thoughts about Him. We could greatly expand our capacity to worship if we would study His Word, memorize the

Psalms, and learn more about intimacy with God. Read great writing on worship. Grow in your understanding of what it means to worship.

One of the worship details we work at very hard here at Harvest is not singing dumb songs. You can't believe how many songs that are called *worship* won't stand up to a close look. Recently, someone on our worship team suggested a particular song that had some good components to it, but one of the lines said, "Jesus, I am so in love with You." Question: Are we *in love* with Jesus? In our day, the expression *in love* means romantic love. Is that what I want to tell Jesus: "Jesus, I'm in love with You"? Is romantic attachment what loving God means? Because, I know that in our world, if you're *in love* with someone, that's a roller-coaster experience. No, what we do is commit to loving a person for a lifetime. That's a commandment. I'm not just in love with my wife—though I am—but I've committed to loving her. So we're not singing about being *in love* with Jesus.

Another song that was noised around here a few years ago also failed the thoughtful love and worship test. It had a number of emotive lines about feeling God's love, but the results it described in terms like "I will rise up like the eagles and I will soar with You and I will . . ." Nonsense! We realized that is not worship. That song is about me; it is not about God. We only sing songs that are about God and directed to Him in a thoughtful and biblical way. I think an element of personal testimony is fine, but when we ascribe worth to God in song, the fact that there's a human participation is nearly irrelevant by the time we're done worshiping. It's about God; not about us. That's the place we want to get to, to be free from myself, fully attentive to God in all His glory. That's the joy of worship; breaking the fetters of self. But this will not happen unless we are willing to be thoughtful in our worship and love for God.

Spirit-worship: Heart and soul

The Great Commandment also includes love and worship with my heart and soul. Earlier in this chapter I described what I call spirit-worship. We should *feel* some things when we worship. Our emotions as well as the rest of us need to be engaged. John Piper has written, "Without the engagement of the heart, we do not really worship. The engagement of the heart in worship is the coming alive of the feelings and emotions and affections of the heart. Where feelings for God are dead, worship is dead."[18]

You ask, "Well, what emotions do you have in mind?" As a preliminary study, here are five emotions described in Scripture that we can feel deeply in worship:

Grief over sin. In Psalm 51:3, David said, **"my sin is ever before me."** He also recognized God does not despise a broken heart.[19] When we come before God in worship, we feel grief over sin; we recognize where we are and where He is, and the gulf between that only He can bridge.

Fear is a second emotion we feel in worship. Psalm 33:8 says, **"Let all the earth fear the LORD; let all the inhabitants of the world stand in awe of him."** As I said earlier, there's a respect and a reverence when we come before God. He is not our buddy. When we take being in His presence for granted, we've begun to lose proper fear of the Lord. If we are never afraid, our view of God is too limited.

Longing is a third emotion that we feel in worship. The Psalms help us locate these feelings. **"My soul longs, yes, faints for the courts of the Lord."**[20] Psalm 42:1 says, **"As the dear pants for flowing streams, so pants my soul for you, O God."** To come to the attitude where you are continually longing for a deeper relationship with Him is something we develop in worship.

Thankfulness and overflowing gratitude saturate authentic worship. Psalm 95:2: **"Let us come into his presence with thanksgiving."** Psalm 100:4 describes the rising tide of grateful worship as God's people come together, **"Enter his gates with thanksgiving, and his courts with praise! Give thanks to him; bless his name!"**

Indescribable joy should be a constant in worship. Psalm 16:11: **"In your presence there is fullness of joy."** Paul is speaking to the church when he writes, **"Rejoice in the Lord always; again I will say, rejoice."**[21]

These are all emotional connections we feel in worship. I hope your heart and soul are rising up to shout, "Yes, I want to feel those things in worship!"

I can only say, "Amen! You should!"

My wife, Kathy, is a great support for me as she faithfully sits in our services and prays for me. In speaking about worship, I've often told people, "How would it work if I said to my wife, 'Well, honey, it's Sunday morning at eleven o'clock and this is always the time when I tell you I love you. Here I am again to tell you that I love you: I love you. Thank you, and I'll see you again next week." I've found most people would agree that strategy is probably not going to work with anyone's wife. Well, that approach to worship does not work with God, either. Just showing up because it's a certain time and saying, "Oh, it's time to tell God I love Him again. I love You, Lord. Are You happy now? I'll see You again next week." That's about as far from authentic worship as you can get.

God wants us to feel some things. He wants total engagement in our worship, including our heart and soul.

You ask, "Well, how can I feel some things?" Well, here are some actions that will help you:

First, drop your guard. God sees you, and the rest of us aren't really watching. We need to stop trying to observe ourselves as we approach God. Quit monitoring your responses: "Oh, oh, I might start feeling something. I'd better be careful here, I don't want to lose control." You should relax a little bit. If tears, smiles, or silence come to you, don't worry about what anyone else is feeling. God's Spirit is working with you in that moment. Let it happen.

Participate. Some people—I see them often when they are first experiencing the impact of exposure to real worship—are not sure *what* to do. Everyone else is singing and praising God but they are in observation mode. Arms crossed, leaning back, externally resisting even as every fiber of their being cries out, "Lean *into* God!" Forget observing; participate. Open your heart and mind; let God bless you and build faith within you. You have to enter in; you have to step forward. You say, "Well, that's hard for me. Do you have any tips for me beyond engaging my heart, soul, and mind in worship?" Yeah, here's the last part Jesus mentioned that we need to engage when we love and worship God: worship with your strength.

Strong worship

God has given us some physical capacities that help us worship. For example, the Bible says, **"Clap your hands, all peoples."**[22] The *all* doesn't really leave anyone out, does it? It always amazes me that some people clap every chance they get in a service *except* when we're worshiping. "Oh, I'll clap for good news during the announcements or after someone shares a great testimony, but I'm not clapping for Jesus. I'm not clapping in the songs of praise. Let the other people clap, I'm not as into it as they are."

Well, why aren't you? What exactly is your deal? Do you think God's up in heaven, going, "I love him, he's so careful about not worshiping Me too much. He never gets carried away. She's always under control." Yeah, I don't think God is saying that! You can clap your hands. Apply your strength to worship.

Here's another physical thing you can do: raise your hands. You say, "Oh, I'd feel so uncomfortable doing that. Is raising hands even biblical?" Paul said, **"I desire then that in every place the men should pray, lifting holy hands . . ."**[23] I can't explain it to you, but there's something that happens—it's like opening my heart when I lift up my hands. You say, "Oh, I don't know if I could do that." Why don't you start by simply holding your hands open before you in worship? That's a good place for you to start.

And let's not forget that I also have my voice. Psalm 47:1 says, **"Clap your hands, all peoples! Shout to God with loud songs of joy!"** Or as an older translation puts it, **"Shout unto God with the voice of triumph."**[24] God forgive us for our soft, almost inaudible little, "I love You, Lord, and I lift my voice. . . ." *Lifting* implies volume; praise involves elevated sound. Whispering is not more inherently worshipful than shouting. You might say, "Well, James, I don't have a voice as loud as you." Well, then, lift your voice within the parameters of how God has made you. If you have a quiet voice, just max yourself out.

Don't you love it when you're in church beside somebody who is singing to God at the top of his lungs—completely off key? Let me tell you something: God loves that guy. We may not appreciate his voice, but it's the one God gave him! Why *wouldn't* God delight in hearing it used to praise Him? Bring some strength to singing with your whole heart to the Lord.

And now we're going to the edge. So I have my hands and my voice for worship; the Bible also talks about praising God with the dance. So you have your feet, too. This might start with tapping your feet, but you may also find yourself shifting weight with the music or message. Now, until we can work out something that will work together—I know there are some churches where people just run up and down the aisles—Harvest isn't that place. But you and I don't have to have our feet in concrete. You can feel a little free and enter into worship. The physical expressions— these are things that help our spirit worship God. I'll say it again: too many of us only know about truth-worship, and don't know about singing to God from our spirit. Spirit communicating and communing with Spirit—listen, there's power there. As Jesus said to His disciples, **"If you know these things, blessed are you if you do them."**[25] The sincerity and authenticity of all the disciplines we have looked at in these pages starts and ends with worship. God's presence will drive you to practice them more faithfully, and as you make progress you will find yourself drawn into deeper and deeper worship.

I trust this tour of the classic and basic spiritual disciplines of a sincere faith has been encouraging and motivating for you. Now, don't go out and ask the next three people you meet, "What do you think? Am I authentic?" They will probably comment on what you're wearing, and that might not go well. Strangers will eventually let you know if you are an authentic person—you won't have to ask. Those who really know you will probably use other words. If they are wise, they will want to encourage you and challenge you at the same time. "Hey, I can tell you're making some changes. I *like* it. Keep it up!" Ultimately, your efforts (and even failures along the way) to become a more and more genuine follower of Jesus Christ will be affirmed by His Spirit working in you. The disciplines will improve your capacity to "hear" what God is saying, not only through His Word but through other means He may use. **"The Spirit himself bears witness with our spirit that we are children of God."**[1]

People "read" us all the time. Shockingly, our Master gave them permission to evaluate our performance. Jesus said, **"A new commandment I give to you, that you love one another: just as I have loved you, you also are to love one another. By this all people will know that you are my disciples, if you have love for one another."**[2] How many people could stroll through your life and mine and conclude that they are sure we love Jesus because of the way we love other Christians? Does the quality of our love bear the characteristics of authenticity? Do we love like Jesus loves?

The new commandment that Jesus gave and the Great Command-ment that He endorsed work hand in hand in our lives. Jesus had already declared the life's bottom line had to be His Father's standard: **"The most important** (commandment) **is, 'Hear, O Israel: The Lord our God, the Lord is one. And you shall love the Lord your God with all your heart and with all your soul and with all your mind and with all your strength.' The second is this: 'You shall love your neighbor as your-self.' There is no other commandment greater than these."**[3]

These commandments are not at all in tension with each other. The great one *includes* the new one. Jesus was saying, "Your authenticity will be determined by the way you treat each other. And by the way you treat God." It all starts with learning to love God with our whole selves, as we discussed. The spiritual disciplines are part of the arsenal of practical actions we can take to make progress in sincere faith.

Perhaps a word we haven't given enough attention to in the subtitle of this book is *developing*. But it's been on my mind throughout. What you have been seeking to do and will hopefully continue to do when you close this book is *develop* the disciplines of a sincere faith. If I could pray one specific, visualized prayer for you as you finish this book, it would be this:

Father, I thank You for this loved one of Yours who has just met the challenge of simply reading through this book. Please bless them in and as a result of their effort. Lord, a year from now may this reader, wherever they understand themselves to be at this moment, see significant progress in one or more of these disciplines. May his or her times in Your Word be deeply satisfying and challenging, marked by grow-ing hunger to listen to You. May they be able to look back on significant answers to prayer as they cry out to You. And may they have experienced the joy of a fast that brought clarity to matters in their lives that Your Spirit wanted to bring to their attention. And may they not settle for superficial fellowship but plunge into the deep end of the pool, where the sense of depth is nourishing to the soul. May their commitment to practical, unheralded service bring a new awareness to them that we can spend ourselves joyfully for You. And finally, may they have discovered the continual joy of exposure to Your glory in wholehearted worship, coming before You in spirit and truth. In all these things, may they realize they haven't come very far, but they have made real progress. As they see development in themselves, may they also realize that You are pleased with them. Thank You for being always ready to develop in us the spiritual disciplines of a sincere faith in You, causing us **"both to will and to work for your good pleasure."**[4] *We are eternally grateful in Jesus' name, Amen.*

Introduction

1. Colossians 1:15–17
2. John 21:19, 23
3. 1 Peter 2:21
4. 1 Timothy 4:15–16, italics mine
5. Philippians 2:12–13
6. John 16:33

Chapter One—Seven Habits of Highly Hypocritical People

1. Luke 22:63
2. Deuteronomy 6:6–9
3. Matthew 15:8
4. James 1:22–25
5. Matthew 23:13
6. Luke 10:21
7. 2 Corinthians 11:3 NKJV
8. If you're following along in your Bible, you may notice that verse 14 is missing. This is what Bible scholars call a textual variant. There is more manuscript evidence for the Bible than any fifty pieces of ancient literature put together. But there are a handful of places in the New Testament where there is disagreement about what belongs in the text. This is an example. Some Bibles (KJV, NKJV) include the verse. New American Standard includes it in brackets. The NIV skipped it. The ESV puts it in a marginal note at the bottom. Here is why this doesn't matter: because the debate is only whether it was in the original writing of Matthew. The very same thing is said in Mark 12:40; Luke 20:47. The bottom line? The only thing that is being debated is whether it belongs in the book of Matthew. So I'm just going to include it. It was part of His judgment upon Pharisees.
9. Matthew 23:14 NKJV

10. James 1:26–27

11. Matthew 23:15

12. 1 Samuel 16:7

13. James 3:2

14. Matthew 23:15

15. Interview with Elizabeth Grice of the *London Daily Telegraph*, May 23, 1998 (http:www.telegraph.uk.com).

16. NKJV

17. Psalm 62:10

18. Matthew 27:24–25

Chapter Two—The Discipline of Personal Bible Study

1. Psalm 1:2–3

2. Psalm 19:7–9

3. NKJV

4. NKJV

5. Romans 1:16–25; Colossians 1:13–20; and Hebrews 1:1–4

6. Psalm 19:8

7. Luke 24:27

8. Luke 24:32

9. Psalm 19:8b

10. Galatians 6:7

11. Psalm 19:9

12. NKJV

13. Matthew 5:6

14. Matthew 13

15. Psalm 119:105

16. James 1:23–25

17. James 1:25

18. Psalm 119:11

19. Proverbs 29:22

20. Hebrews 10:24

Chapter Three—The Discipline of Personal Prayer

1. Ephesians 3:20

2. KJV

3. Luke 11:1

4. John 1:14

5. Romans 8:34

6. Psalm 23:3

7. Exodus 3:13–15 describes how God assigned this name to Himself, which is related to "I AM."

8. Exodus 20:7

9. Jeremiah 23:5–6

10. Titus 3:5

11. Leviticus 20:8

12. Ezekiel 48:35

13. Judges 6:24

14. Philippians 4:4–7

15. Ephesians 3:20

16. John 14:27; 16:33

17. Exodus 17:15

18. Matthew 6:10

19. Luke 22:42

20. John 18:11

21. 1 Peter 5:7

22. Mark 11:24

23. 1 John 5:15

24. John 15:7

25. James 4:2–3

26. Hebrews 4:14–16

27. 2 Peter 3:9 NKJV

28. Matthew 6:12

29. Matthew 5:23–24

30. Matthew 6:13 NKJV. ESV, and others include the phrase in a footnote.

Chapter Four—The Discipline of Fasting

1. Matthew 17:21 NKJV

2. Wilbur Reese, *$3.00 Worth of God* (Elgin, IL: Judson Press, 1971).

3. NASB

4. Philippians 3:19 NKJV

5. Norman Grubb, *Rees Howells: Intercessor* (Fort Washington, PA: Christian Literature Crusade, rev. 1988), chapter 8.

6. 1 Peter 2:11

7. John Piper, *Hunger for God* (Wheaton: Crossway Books, 1997), 93.

8. Richard Foster, *Celebration of Discipline* (San Francisco, Harper & Row, 1988), 56.

9. Zechariah 7:5

10. Colossians 3:1

11. Acts 9:9

12. Ezra 10:6

13. Esther 4:16
14. Joel 2:15
15. John 10:10
16. Romans 12:1–2
17. Psalm 84:10
18. Psalm 84:10–11

Chapter Five—The Discipline of Fellowship

1. John 2:25 NKJV
2. Jerry Cook and Stanley C. Baldwin, *Love, Acceptance, and Commitment: Being Christian in a Non-Christian World* (Ventura, CA.: Regal, 2009), 14-15.
3. This in direct violation of the principles in Philippians 2:1–5.
4. ESV
5. NKJV
6. James 3:2
7. 1 Corinthians 10:13
8. 2 Corinthians 8:1
9. 2 Corinthians 8:2–4
10. Galatians 1:23–24
11. Galatians 2:2
12. Galatians 2:9
13. Galatians 2:9
14. Philippians 1:5
15. The NIV tries to cover both bases by making the verse, "I want to know Christ and the power of his resurrection and the fellowship of sharing in his sufferings, becoming like him in his death."
16. See Galatians 6:2
17. See Ephesians 4:1

Chapter Six—The Discipline of Service

1. Mark 10:45
2. Philippians 4:4–7
3. Matthew 25:21, 23
4. 2 Timothy 2:2
5. See John 2:4; 7:30; 8:20
6. John 13:21
7. Matthew 26:21
8. Matthew 26:23
9. Luke 22:21
10. Mark 14:21
11. John 13:21

12. Matthew 26:24
13. John 13:3–5
14. Luke 22:8–13
15. Hebrews 12:2
16. John 13:17

Chapter Seven—The Discipline of Worship

1. John 13:17
2. Isaiah 55:9
3. Exodus 20:3
4. Matthew 6:19–21
5. John 3:16
6. John 6:37
7. John 1:12
8. Romans 3:11
9. Luke 19:10
10. Matthew 18:12–14; Luke 15:3–7
11. 2 Peter 3:9
12. John 4:23
13. Ephesians 2:1–10
14. John 4:24
15. 1 Corinthians 14:24, emphasis mine
16. Quoted by Elsie Washington in Black Issues Book Review, May/June 2002, 57; www.PreachingToday.com. Ilyasah's autobiography is entitled *Growing Up X* (New York: One World/Ballantine, 2003).
17. James 4:8
18. John Piper, *Desiring God*, rev. ed.(Colorado Springs: Multnomah, 2011), 87–88, emphasis Piper.
19. Psalm 51:17
20 Psalm 84:1
21. Philippians 4:4
22. Psalm 47:1
23. 1 Timothy 2:8, also Psalm 28:2; 119:48
24. Psalm 47:1 KJV
25. John 13:17

Conclusion

1. Romans 8:16
2. John 13:34–35
3. Mark 12:29–31
4. Philippians 2:13

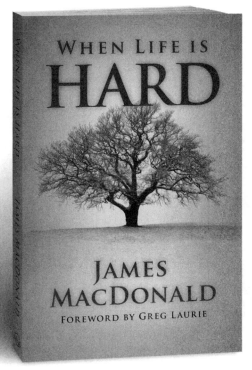

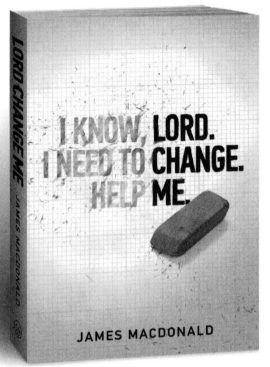